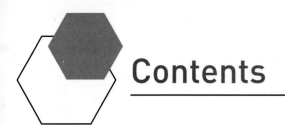

Contents

KV-385-755

Contents

GEOMETRY AND MEASURES

HIGHER 2

Practice Book

MASTERING

MATHEMATICS

FOR
EDEXCEL GCSE

Practice • Reinforcement • Progress

Assessment Consultant and Editor: **Keith Pledger**

Keith Pledger, Gareth Cole, and Joe Petran

Series Editor: Roger Porkess

HODDER
EDUCATION
AN HACHETTE UK COMPANY

Although every effort has been made to ensure that website addresses are correct at time of going to press, Hodder Education cannot be held responsible for the content of any website mentioned. It is sometimes possible to find a relocated web page by typing in the address of the home page for a website in the URL window of your browser.

Orders: please contact Bookpoint Ltd, 130 Milton Park, Abingdon, Oxon OX14 4SB. Telephone: (44) 01235 827720. Fax: (44) 01235 400454. Lines are open 9.00–17.00, Monday to Saturday, with a 24-hour message answering service. Visit our website at www.hoddereducation.co.uk.

© Keith Pledger, Gareth Cole, Joe Petran 2016

First published in 2016 by

Hodder Education

An Hachette UK Company,

50 Victoria Embankment

London EC4Y 0DZ

Impression number	5	4	3	2	1
Year	2020	2019	2018	2017	2016

Cover photo © agsandrew - Fotolia.com

Illustrations by Integra

Typeset in India by Integra Software Services Pvt. Ltd., Pondicherry

Printed in Great Britain by CPI Group (UK) Ltd, Croydon CR0 4YY

A catalogue record for this title is available from the British Library.

ISBN 9781471874499

How to get the most from this book

Introduction

This book is part of the Mastering Mathematics for Edexcel GCSE series and supports the textbook by providing lots of extra practice questions for the Higher tier.

This Practice Book is structured to match the Higher Student's Book and is likewise organised by key areas of the specification: Number, Algebra, Geometry & Measures and Statistics & Probability. Every chapter in this book accompanies its corresponding chapter from the textbook, with matching titles for ease of use.

Please note: the 'Moving On' units in the Student's Book cover prior knowledge only, so do not have accompanying chapters in this Practice Book. For this reason, although the running order of the Practice Book follows the Student's Book, you may notice that some Strand/Unit numbers appear to be missing, or do not start at '1'.

Progression through each chapter

Chapters include a range of questions that increase in difficulty as you progress through the exercise. There are three levels of difficulty across the Student's Books and Practice Books in this series. These are denoted by shaded spots on the right hand side of each page. Levels broadly reflect GCSE Maths grades as follows:

Low difficulty   GCSE Maths grades 1–3   ●○○

Medium difficulty   GCSE Maths grades 4–6   ●●○

High difficulty   GCSE Maths grades 7–9   ●●●

You might wish to start at the beginning of each chapter and work through so you can see how you are progressing.

Question types

There is also a range of question types included in each chapter, which are denoted by codes to the left hand side of the question or sub-question where they appear. These are examples of the types of question that you will need to practice in readiness for the GCSE Maths Higher exam.

PS Practising skills

These questions are all about building and mastering the essential techniques that you need to succeed.

DF Developing fluency

These give you practice of using your skills for a variety of purposes and contexts, building your confidence to tackle any type of question.

PB Problem solving

These give practice of using your problem solving skills in order to tackle more demanding problems in the real world, in other subjects and within Maths itself.

Next to any question, including the above question types, you may also see the below code. This means that it is an exam-style question

ES Exam style

This question reflects the language, style and wording of a question that you might see in your GCSE Maths Higher exam.

Answers

There are answers to every question within the book on our website.

Please visit: www.hoddereducation.co.uk/MasteringmathsforEdexcelGCSE

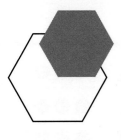

Number Strand 2 Using our number system
Unit 8 Recurring decimals

PS ▸ PRACTISING SKILLS   **DF** ▸ DEVELOPING FLUENCY   **PB** ▸ PROBLEM SOLVING   **ES** ▸ EXAM-STYLE

PS **1** Which of these fractions can be written as a recurring decimal?

   a $\dfrac{1}{3}$

   b $\dfrac{3}{6}$

   c $\dfrac{1}{15}$

   d $\dfrac{7}{20}$

   e $\dfrac{2}{13}$

PS **2** Convert these recurring decimals into fractions.

   a $0.\dot{7}$

   b $0.\dot{5}$

   c $0.\dot{1}\dot{3}$

   d $0.4\dot{5}$

   e $0.\dot{1}5\dot{1}$

DF **3** Write these recurring decimals as fractions.

   a $0.\dot{4}$

   b $0.0\dot{4}$

   c $0.00\dot{4}$

   d $0.0\dot{1}0\dot{4}$

   e $5.000\dot{4}$

DF **4** **a** Write down the recurring decimals for $\dfrac{1}{13}, \dfrac{3}{13}, \dfrac{4}{13}, \dfrac{9}{13}, \dfrac{10}{13}, \dfrac{12}{13}$.

b Write down the recurring decimals for $\dfrac{2}{13}, \dfrac{5}{13}, \dfrac{6}{13}, \dfrac{7}{13}, \dfrac{8}{13}, \dfrac{11}{13}$.

c Explain what you notice between the two sets of fractions.

PB **5** Seventeenths also have a pattern of repeating digits in their recurring decimals. There are 16 digits in the pattern.
Work out the order of the digits. You must show your working.

PB **ES** **6** Given that $0.\dot{4} = \dfrac{4}{9}$, express the recurring decimal $0.6\dot{4}$ as a fraction.

PB **ES** **7** Explain why $9.\dot{9} = 10$.

PB **ES** **8** Explain why any fraction of the form $\dfrac{1}{p}$ where p is a prime number

can be written as a recurring decimal when p is not 2 or 5, and why the number of digits in the recurring pattern is always less than p. Give an example.

DF **9** Convert each of these recurring decimals into a fraction in its simplest form.

a $0.\dot{5}$

b $0.7\dot{5}$

c $0.0\dot{2}\dot{5}$

d $0.3\dot{2}3\dot{5}$

e $5.1\dot{2}0\dot{5}$

Number Strand 3 Accuracy Unit 8 Calculating with upper and lower bounds

PS PRACTISING SKILLS   **DF** DEVELOPING FLUENCY   **PB** PROBLEM SOLVING   **ES** EXAM-STYLE

PS **1** Write down the number that is halfway between:

  a 5 and 6

  b 6.5 and 6.6

  c 17.67 and 17.68

  d 2.362 and 2.363

  e 10 and 10.0001

PS **2** Write down the lower bound and the upper bound for these measurements.

  a The length of a pencil is 14 cm to the nearest centimetre.

  b The length of a race is 100 m measured to the nearest centimetre.

  c The weight of a chocolate bar is 75 g to the nearest gram.

  d The weight of a bag of compost is 25 kg to the nearest 100 grams.

  e The capacity of a bottle of milk is 1 litre measured to the nearest 10 ml.

PS **ES** **3** Judy buys four packs of butter. Each pack of butter weighs 250 g to the nearest gram.

  Work out the upper and lower bounds for the total weight of butter that Judy buys.

DF **4** Raphael paints pictures. He charges £150 per square metre for every painting he sells. He paints a rectangular picture that has a length of 1.2 m and a width of 80 cm. Both measurements are correct to the nearest centimetre.

  Work out the upper and lower bounds of the cost of this picture.

DF **ES** **5** The circumference of the Earth around the equator is 24 900 miles correct to the nearest 10 miles.

  a Work out the upper and lower bounds of the diameter of the Earth.

  b What assumption have you made in carrying out this calculation?

DF **6** Rhodri has a ladder that is 10m long measured correct to the
nearest 2cm. The base of the ladder has to be 3m measured
to the nearest 5cm from the base of a wall.

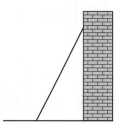

Find the upper bound and the lower bound of the height the ladder
can reach up the wall.

PB **7** Peter cycled to work. His average speed was 4.8m/s correct to
ES   1 decimal place. It took him 20 minutes correct to the nearest minute.

   a Calculate the lower bound of the distance that Peter travelled
   to work.

Peter took a different route home from work. He cycled a distance of 6.2km
correct to 1 decimal place. It took him 19 minutes correct to the nearest minute.

   b Calculate the upper bound of Peter's average speed in m/s for his
   journey home.

PB **8** Mary ran a distance of 200m in a time of 26.35 seconds.
ES   The distance of 200m was measured to the nearest 10 centimetres.
         The time of 26.35 seconds was measured to the nearest hundredth
         of a second.

   a Work out the upper and lower bounds for Mary's average speed in
   metres per second.

   b Write down an appropriate estimate for Mary's average speed.

PB **9** The average fuel consumption (f) of a car, in kilometres
ES   per litre, is given by the formula $f = \dfrac{d}{u}$ where d is the distance
         travelled in kilometres and u is the fuel used in litres.

Jill travels 430km and uses 52.3 litres of fuel. The 430 is written correct to
3 significant figures. The 52.3 is written correct to one decimal place.

Work out the value of f to a suitable degree of accuracy. You must show
all of your working and give a reason for your final answer.

PB **10** There are roadworks on a motorway for 3.7 miles correct to the
ES   nearest tenth of a mile. There is a speed restriction of exactly 50mph
          on this section of motorway. Mandeep takes 4.5 minutes correct to
          the nearest 10 seconds to drive this section of motorway.

Does Mandeep exceed the speed restriction? You must explain
your answer.

Number Strand 5 Percentages Unit 8 Growth and decay

PS PRACTISING SKILLS   **DF** DEVELOPING FLUENCY   **PB** PROBLEM SOLVING   **ES** EXAM-STYLE

PS **1** Write the following percentage changes as decimal multipliers. ●●○

    a 20% increase

    b 5% decrease

    c 17.5% increase

    d 2.5% decrease

PS **2** Write the following multipliers as percentage increases or decreases. ●●○

    a 1.05

    b 0.9

    c 1.025

    d 0.875

    e 2

PS **3** Rafa invests £500 in an account that pays 3.5% compound interest. ●●●

    a Work out how much money Rafa had in the account after four years.

    b How many years would it take for the amount in the account to first exceed £1000?

DF **ES** **4** Rachel invests £250 in a bank account for five years. The bank pays compound interest at an annual rate of 4.5% for the first year and 3.0% for each of the other four years. ●●●

How much interest did Rachel earn in total in the five years?

DF **ES** **5** Giovanni invests £12 000 in a variable rate compound interest account for three years. The interest rates are 2% for the first year and 3.5% for the second year and 5% for the third year. ●●●

Work out the value of Giovanni's investment at the end of the three years.

DF
ES
6 Didi bought a car for £10 000. It depreciated 15% in the first year she owned the car and 10% in each subsequent year.

    a Find the value of the car at the end of the third year.

    b How many years will it take for the value of Didi's car take to drop below £4500?

PB
ES
7 A cell reproduces by splitting into two every hour.
There is one cell at the beginning.
There are two cells after one hour.
There are four cells after two hours.
In hour $(n + 1)$ there are twice as many cells as in hour n.

    a Find the number of cells after 10 hours. Give your answer as a power of 2.

After 24 hours three quarters of the cells were removed.

    b How many cells were left? Give your answer as a power of 2.

PB
ES
8 A scientist is studying some rabbits. The rabbits have a disease that kills the rabbits. A colony of 160 of these rabbits was reduced to 90 in two days. The rabbit population is decreasing exponentially.
Work out how many of the original population of 160 rabbits will still be alive after seven days.

PB
ES
9 Rhiannon is investigating the population growth of mice held in captivity. There were 120 mice at the start of month 1. There were 240 mice at the start of month 3. The population of mice is increasing exponentially.
Work out how many mice Rhiannon thinks there will be at the start of month 6.

PB
ES
10 Bill has a beehive. The number of bees in his beehive is decreasing. Bill counts the number of bees in his hive at the start of week 4 and week 6. Here are his results:

Week	Number of bees
4	1600
6	1200

Bill assumes that the population of bees is decreasing exponentially.
How many bees were in the hive at the start of week 1?

Number Strand 6 Ratio and proportion
Unit 6 Formulating equations to solve proportion problems

PS PRACTISING SKILLS   DF DEVELOPING FLUENCY   PB PROBLEM SOLVING   ES EXAM-STYLE

PS **1** Write the following relationships using the 'proportional to' sign ($\propto$). ●●●

    a y varies as x

    b y varies as the square of x

    c y varies inversely as x

    d y varies as the square root of x

    e y varies as the cube of x

    f y varies inversely as the square of x

PS **2** Given that $y = 40$ when $x = 10$, write an equation to show each of these relationships. ●●●

    a y varies as x

    b y varies as the square of x

    c y varies inversely as x

    d y varies as the square root of x

    e y varies as the cube of x

    f y varies inversely as the square of x

PS **ES** **3** p varies as the square of t. When $p = 75$, $t = 5$. Find the value of p when $t = 8$. ●●●

PS **ES** **4** r varies inversely as the cube of s. When $r = 5$, $s = 2$. Find the value of r when $s = \frac{1}{2}$. ●●●

DF **ES** **5** The time taken for the pendulum of a clock to make one complete swing is proportional to the square root of the length of the pendulum. ●●●

When the pendulum is 50 cm long the time for one complete swing is one second.

How long is the pendulum when one complete swing takes two seconds?

DF
ES

6 Sylvia carries out an experiment on how long a liquid takes to cool in a freezer.

She records the time (m) in minutes and temperature (t) in degrees Celsius. Here are her results:

Time m	1	4	9	x
Temperature t	24	12	8	4.8

Sylvia thinks that t varies inversely as the square root of m.

Find the value of x when the temperature is 4.8°C.

PB
ES

7 The resistance to motion of a car is directly proportional the square of the speed of the car. When the speed of the car is 25 metres per second the resistance to motion is 80 000 N.

Find the resistance to motion when the speed of the car is 108 km per hour.

PB
ES

8 In the winter a farmer feeds his cattle with hay each day. The number of days, d, the hay will last is inversely proportional to the number of cows, c. The farmer has enough hay to feed 120 cows for 30 days. The farmer has a herd of 75 cows.

For how many days will the farmer be able to feed his cows?

PB
ES

9 Paul plays in a band. The loudness of the music varies inversely as the square of the distance from the band. Paul measures the loudness of his band as 115 decibels at a distance of 4 m.

Paul's band are playing at a wedding. They have to stop playing if the loudness is more than 100 decibels at a distance of 5 m.

Explain if Paul's band have to stop playing.

PB
ES

10 The pressure, P, on a diver as she dives under the water is proportional to the square of her depth, d, below the surface of the water. She dives to 10 m below the surface of the water.

Explain why she needs to dive a further $10(\sqrt{2} - 1)$ m for the pressure to double.

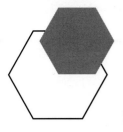

Number Strand 7 Number properties Unit 7 Fractional indices

PS PRACTISING SKILLS **DF** DEVELOPING FLUENCY **PB** PROBLEM SOLVING **ES** EXAM-STYLE

PS **1** Write the following as roots.

    a $5^{\frac{1}{2}}$

    b $4^{\frac{1}{3}}$

    c $3^{\frac{1}{4}}$

    d $8^{\frac{1}{2}}$

    e $10^{\frac{1}{5}}$

    f $6^{\frac{1}{5}}$

PS **2** Write the following using indices.

    a $\sqrt{7}$

    b $\sqrt[3]{9}$

    c $\sqrt[3]{4}$

    d $\sqrt{5}$

    e $\sqrt[6]{5}$

    f $\sqrt[7]{2}$

PS **3** Find the value of each of these.

    a $81^{\frac{1}{2}}$

    b $8^{\frac{1}{3}}$

    c $256^{\frac{1}{4}}$

    d $169^{\frac{1}{2}}$

    e $216^{\frac{1}{3}}$

    f $625^{\frac{1}{4}}$

DF **4** Write the following using roots.

    a $5^{\frac{3}{2}}$

    b $7^{\frac{2}{3}}$

    c $6^{\frac{3}{4}}$

    d $10^{\frac{5}{3}}$

    e $10^{\frac{2}{5}}$

    f $5^{\frac{5}{2}}$

DF **5** Write the following using indices.

    a $\sqrt{2^3}$

    b $(\sqrt[4]{3})^3$

    c $\sqrt[3]{5^7}$

    d $\sqrt[4]{7^5}$

    e $(\sqrt[3]{2})^5$

    f $(\sqrt[5]{2})^9$

DF **6** Find the value of each of these.

    a $36^{\frac{3}{2}}$

    b $8^{\frac{2}{3}}$

    c $256^{\frac{3}{4}}$

    d $4^{\frac{5}{2}}$

    e $27^{\frac{5}{3}}$

    f $625^{\frac{3}{4}}$

DF **7** Write the following as roots.

    a $3^{-\frac{1}{2}}$

    b $4^{-\frac{1}{3}}$

    c $5^{-\frac{3}{4}}$

    d $7^{-\frac{3}{2}}$

    e $9^{-\frac{4}{5}}$

    f $3^{-\frac{2}{5}}$

DF **8** Write the following using indices.

    a $\dfrac{1}{\sqrt{5}}$

    b $\dfrac{1}{\sqrt[4]{7}}$

    c $\dfrac{1}{\sqrt[3]{5^2}}$

    d $\dfrac{1}{(\sqrt{7})^3}$

    e $\dfrac{1}{\sqrt[4]{3^5}}$

    f $\dfrac{1}{(\sqrt[5]{3})^3}$

DF **9** Find the value of each of these.

    a $16^{-\frac{3}{2}}$

    b $64^{-\frac{2}{3}}$

    c $125^{-\frac{5}{3}}$

    d $4^{-\frac{3}{2}}$

    e $27^{-\frac{2}{3}}$

    f $64^{-\frac{5}{6}}$

PB **10** Write the value of each of these as a power of 2.

    a $4 \times 32^{\frac{3}{5}}$

    b $\dfrac{1}{8} \times 64^{\frac{3}{2}}$

    c $8^{-\frac{5}{3}} \times 32^{\frac{2}{5}}$

PB **11** Find the value of n.

    a $\dfrac{1}{\sqrt{8}} = 2^n$

    b $\sqrt[3]{27^2} = 3^n$

    c $(\sqrt[3]{125})^4 = 25^n$

PB **12** **a** Work out $\left(\dfrac{125}{27}\right)^{-\frac{2}{3}}$

ES   **b** Find the value of p in this numeric identity.

      $3 \times 8^{\frac{2}{3}} = 96 \times p^{-\frac{1}{3}}$

Number Strand 7 Number properties Unit 8 Surds

PS — PRACTISING SKILLS   DF — DEVELOPING FLUENCY   PB — PROBLEM SOLVING   ES — EXAM-STYLE

PS **1** Write the following roots in the form $a\sqrt{b}$.

   a $\sqrt{8}$

   b $\sqrt{27}$

   c $\sqrt{20}$

   d $\sqrt{200}$

   e $\sqrt{72}$

   f $\sqrt{63}$

PS **2** Simplify the following roots.

   a $\sqrt{48}$

   b $\sqrt{18}$

   c $\sqrt{54}$

   d $\sqrt{500}$

   e $\sqrt{45}$

   f $\sqrt{125}$

PS **3** Rationalise the denominator of each of these fractions.

   a $\dfrac{3}{\sqrt{2}}$

   b $\dfrac{3}{\sqrt{3}}$

   c $\dfrac{4}{\sqrt{5}}$

   d $\dfrac{20}{\sqrt{10}}$

   e $\dfrac{3}{\sqrt{6}}$

   f $\dfrac{15}{\sqrt{10}}$

DF **4** Write each of the following fractions in its simplest form.

a $\dfrac{2}{\sqrt{2}}$

b $\dfrac{25}{\sqrt{5}}$

c $\dfrac{4\sqrt{3}}{\sqrt{12}}$

d $\dfrac{25}{\sqrt{10}}$

e $\dfrac{3\sqrt{2}}{\sqrt{8}}$

f $\dfrac{3\sqrt{5}}{\sqrt{10}}$

DF **5** Multiply out and simplify the bracketed expressions.

a $(3+\sqrt{2})(3-\sqrt{2})$

b $(3+\sqrt{2})(3+\sqrt{2})$

c $(\sqrt{3}+\sqrt{2})(\sqrt{3}-\sqrt{2})$

d $(\sqrt{3}-\sqrt{2})(\sqrt{3}-\sqrt{2})$

e $(\sqrt{3}+\sqrt{2})^2$

f $(\sqrt{75}+\sqrt{72})(\sqrt{75}-\sqrt{72})$

DF **6** Rationalise the denominator and write the answer as a surd in its simplest form.

a $\dfrac{1}{5+\sqrt{7}}$

b $\dfrac{4}{5-\sqrt{7}}$

c $\dfrac{\sqrt{7}}{5+\sqrt{7}}$

d $\dfrac{1}{\sqrt{7}+\sqrt{5}}$

e $\dfrac{\sqrt{35}}{\sqrt{7}-\sqrt{5}}$

PB
ES
7 Explain why the angle marked x is 60°.

10 cm $\sqrt{75}$ cm

x

PB
ES
8 Explain why the angle marked y is 30°.

$\sqrt{112}$ cm

y

$\sqrt{84}$ cm

PB
ES
9 Squares are drawn on the sides of the right-angled triangle. Work out the perimeter of the right-angled triangle. Give your answer in surd form.

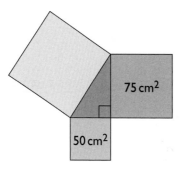

75 cm²

50 cm²

PB
ES
10 PQR is a right-angled triangle. All the measurements are in cm.

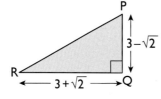

P

$3 - \sqrt{2}$

R

$3 + \sqrt{2}$ Q

a Work out the area of triangle PQR.

b Work out the perimeter of triangle PQR.

Algebra Strand 1 Starting algebra Unit 12 Using indices in algebra

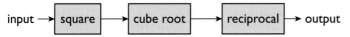

| PS | PRACTISING SKILLS | DF | DEVELOPING FLUENCY | PB | PROBLEM SOLVING | ES | EXAM-STYLE |

PS **ES** **1** Here is an input–output machine.

input → | square | → | cube root | → | reciprocal | → output

a Work out the output, as a power of c, when the input is c.

b Work out the input, as a power of d, when the output is d.

PS **2** Simplify these.

a $(a^2b^3)^{-1} \div ab^2$

b $\sqrt{ab^{-1}} \times \dfrac{1}{\sqrt{a^3b}}$

c $\dfrac{p^3}{q^2} \div \dfrac{q^{-1}}{\sqrt{p}}$

d $\dfrac{\sqrt[3]{p^2}}{q^{-2}} \times \dfrac{(2q)^2}{p^4}$

DF **ES** **3** Simplify these.

a $(2pq^2)^2 \div (4p^3(q^2)^{-1})$

b $\sqrt{(2pq)^3 \times 2pq^{-5}}$

c $\dfrac{a^2b^{\frac{1}{3}} \times a^{-1}b^{\frac{2}{3}}}{ab}$

d $\sqrt[3]{\dfrac{p^2q \times p^5q^3}{pq}}$

PB **ES** **4** The area of this square is the same as the area of this right-angled triangle.

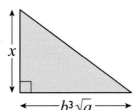

x can be written in the form pa^nb^m.
Find the values of p, n and m.

DF **5** $x = a^2 b^{-\frac{3}{2}}$ $y = a^{\frac{5}{2}} b^2$

ES   **a** Work out the square of xy.

    b Work out the cube of $\dfrac{x}{y}$.

PS **6** Write each of the following as a power of x.

    a $\dfrac{x}{\sqrt{4x^4}}$ **b** $((x^2)^{-5})^{-1}$ **c** $\sqrt[3]{x^{-4}}$

    d $\dfrac{1}{\sqrt{x^3}}$ **e** $\left(\dfrac{x^2}{x^{-3}}\right)^{\frac{1}{2}}$ **f** $\dfrac{\sqrt[3]{x}}{(2x^{-1})^3}$

DF **7** Find the value of n in the following equations.

ES   **a** $\sqrt{p} \times p^n = \dfrac{1}{p}$

    b $\dfrac{q^3}{\sqrt{q} \times q^n} = q^{\frac{5}{2}}$

DF **8** **a** Simplify $(\sqrt{a} - 3\sqrt{b})(2\sqrt{a} + \sqrt{b})$.

ES   **b** Write as a single fraction $\dfrac{2}{\sqrt{n}} + \dfrac{3\sqrt{n}}{4}$.

    c Solve $5^x = \dfrac{1}{125}$.

PB **9** The area of this right-angled triangle is $15\,\text{cm}^2$.

ES   **a** Show that the area of this right-angled triangle can be written as $2\sqrt{a^5 b^3}$.

    b Find an expression, in terms of a and b, for the length of the hypotenuse.

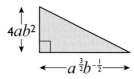

$4ab^2$

$a^{\frac{3}{2}} b^{-\frac{1}{2}}$

DF **10** **a** Simplify $2a^3 b^{-1} \times \dfrac{5}{ab^2}$.

ES   **b** $x^{2.5} \times x^{n-1} = \dfrac{1}{\sqrt{x}}$. Work out the value of n.

Algebra Strand 1 Starting algebra Unit 13 Manipulating more expressions and equations

PS — PRACTISING SKILLS   **DF** — DEVELOPING FLUENCY   **PB** — PROBLEM SOLVING   **ES** — EXAM-STYLE

PS **1** Expand and simplify these.

    a $(x + 7)(x + 9)$

    b $(x - 5)(x + 11)$

    c $(x - 4)(x - 5)$

    d $(2x + 3)(5x - 2)$

    e $(3 - x)(5 + 2x)$

    f $(x - 6)(7 - 2x)$

PB **ES** **2** $(3x + 1)(ax + b) = 6x^2 - 7x - 3$

    Work out the values and a and b.

DF **ES** **3** **a** Expand $(x - 1)(x - 2)(x - 3)$

    b $(x + 3)(x - a)(x - b) = x^3 + 2x^2 - 23x - 60$. Work out the values of a and b.

PB **ES** **4** It takes Asif 15 minutes more than Waqar to travel a distance of 20 miles. It takes Waqar t hours to travel this distance of 20 miles. Work out the difference, in terms of t, in their average speeds.

DF **ES** **5** Solve these.

    a $\dfrac{x}{4} + \dfrac{x}{5} = 1$

    b $\dfrac{x - 1}{2} - \dfrac{x + 1}{3} = 6$

PB **ES** **6** The area of this right-angled triangle is $15\,\text{cm}^2$. Work out the perimeter of the triangle.

$(2x - 1)\,\text{cm}$

$(x + 3)\,\text{cm}$

PS **7** Expand and simplify these.

   a $(\sqrt{x} - 1)(\sqrt{x} + 1)$

   b $(x - \sqrt{3})(x + 2\sqrt{3})$

   c $(\sqrt{x} + \sqrt{5})(\sqrt{x} + \sqrt{10})$

   d $(2\sqrt{x} + \sqrt{3})^2$

DF **ES** **8** Simplify these.

   a $\dfrac{(6a-2b)}{(2a+b)(3a-b)}$

   b $\dfrac{p^2 - pq - 2q^2}{p^2 - q^2}$

DF **ES** **9** Simplify these.

   a $\dfrac{(u+v)^2 - w^2}{(w+v)^2 - u^2}$

   b $\dfrac{b^2 - ac - ab - bc}{c^2 - ac + ab - bc}$

DF **10** Write the following as powers of x.

   a $10\left(x + \dfrac{1}{x}\right) = 29$

   b $\dfrac{10x+1}{2x-1} - \dfrac{3x+8}{x+1} = 2$

PB **ES** **11** The diagram shows a net of an open metal box. The net is cut from a sheet of dimensions $(x + 2)$ cm by $(x - 1)$ cm. A square of side 1 cm is cut out at each corner. The net is then folded along the dotted lines to form the box.

   If the volume of the box is 70 cm³, work out the dimensions of the sheet of metal.

DF **ES** **12** $x = 1 + \dfrac{p}{p-q}$ $y = 2 - \dfrac{3q}{p+q}$. Find

   a $\dfrac{x}{y}$

   b $\dfrac{3}{x} + \dfrac{1}{y}$

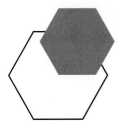

Algebra Strand 1 Starting algebra Unit 14 Rearranging more formulae

PS PRACTISING SKILLS   **DF** DEVELOPING FLUENCY   **PB** PROBLEM SOLVING   **ES** EXAM-STYLE

PS **1** Make the letter shown in brackets the subject of each formula. ●●○

   a $b = a + (n - 1)d$ (n)

   b $e = \dfrac{1}{2}mc^2$ (c)

   c $t = w\sqrt{ag}$ (g)

   d $s = ut + \dfrac{1}{2}at^2$ (a)

PS
ES **2** Here is a prism. The cross section is in the shape of a trapezium. ●●○

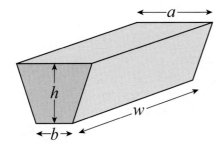

The volume, V, of the prism is given by the formula $V = \dfrac{w}{2}(a + b)h$ where h is the height, w is the length, and a and b are the widths of the top and bottom of the trapezium.

   a Make b the subject of the formula.

   b Find b when $V = 450$, $a = 12$, $h = 5$ and $w = 10$.

DF **3** Make a the subject of the formula $\cos A = \dfrac{b^2 + c^2 - a^2}{2bc}$. ●●○

ES
PB **4** The curved surface area, A, of a cone is given by the ●●○

ES   formula $A = \pi r\sqrt{h^2 + r^2}$ where h is the height and r is the radius of the cone.

   a Make h the subject of the formula.

   b Find h when $A = 550$ and $r = 10$. Take $\pi = 3.14$. Give your answer to three significant figures.

DF **ES**

5 Make w the subject of the formula $T = w + \dfrac{wv^2}{gx}$.

PB **ES**

6 A wire L metres long is stretched between two points. The points are at the same level and are d metres apart. The sag, s metres, in the middle of the wire is given by the formula $s = \sqrt{\dfrac{3d(L-d)}{8}}$

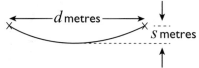

a Rearrange the formula to make L the subject.

b Work out the length of wire that gives a sag of 0.6 m when the two points are 16 m apart.

DF **ES**

7 Make k the subject of the formula $T = 2\pi\sqrt{\dfrac{h^2 + k^2}{2gh}}$.

PB **ES**

8 The total resistance, R ohms, of two resistors in parallel is given by $\dfrac{1}{R} = \dfrac{1}{x} + \dfrac{1}{y}$ where x and y are the resistances, in ohms, of the two resistors.

a Make y the subject of the formula.

b Find y when $x = 2\dfrac{1}{3}$ ohms and $R = 2\dfrac{1}{4}$ ohms.

DF **ES**

9 **a** $x = a + \sqrt{b(x-a)}$. Find x in terms of a and b only.

b Make p the subject of $A = \sqrt{\dfrac{p^2 - 2q^2}{2p^2 + q^2}}$.

DF **ES**

10 $E = 2c\left(1 + \dfrac{1}{m}\right)$ and $E = 3k\left(1 - \dfrac{2}{m}\right)$.

Express m in terms of c and k only.

PB **ES**

11 An arithmetic sequence is formed by adding d to the previous term. If the first term is a, the sum, S, of the first n terms is given by the formula $S = \dfrac{n}{2}\big[2a + (n-1)d\big]$.

a Make d the subject of this formula.

b 25 is the first term of an arithmetic sequence. The sum of the first 32 terms is 56. Find d.

DF **ES**

12 Make d the subject of $A = \sqrt{\dfrac{2v^2d}{g} + \dfrac{d^2}{4}} - \dfrac{d}{2}$.

Algebra Strand 2 Sequences
Unit 7 Other sequences

PS — PRACTISING SKILLS   **DF** — DEVELOPING FLUENCY   **PB** — PROBLEM SOLVING   **ES** — EXAM-STYLE

ES
PS **1** A sequence is formed by doubling the previous term and subtracting 4.

    a Find the 5th term if the first term is 1.

    b Find the 5th term if the first term is 2.

    c Find the 5th term if the first term is 3.

    d Find the 5th term if the first term is 4.

PB
ES **2** Nathan has 250 shares in a company. The shares cost Nathan £1.80 each five years ago. Each year the value of the shares increased by 10%.

    a Work out the total value of Nathan's shares now.

    The value of the shares continues to increase by 10% each year.

    b In what year will the total value of Nathan's shares first be over £1000?

PB
ES **3** Sequence A is formed by adding 1 to the previous term then multiplying by 2. Sequence B is formed by subtracting 2 from the previous term then adding 50. Sequence C is formed by subtracting 5 from the previous term then squaring the result.

    Denzil says that if the first term of each sequence is 8, the 6th term of sequence A is greater than the 6th terms of the other two sequences. Is Denzil right?

DF **4** 5 is the first term of a geometric progression. The common ratio is $\sqrt{3}$.

ES   **a** Write down the first five terms of this geometric progression.

    b The even numbered terms form a different geometric progression. Find the common ratio of this geometric progression.

PS **5** Write down the next two terms of each of these sequences.

    a 81, 27, 9, ...

    b 1, $2\sqrt{2}$, 8, $16\sqrt{2}$, ...

    c 5, 1, 0.2, 0.04, ...

    d For each of the sequences above, write down
        i the common ratio
        ii the 10th term.

PB
ES
6 The rule for a sequence is given by $u_{n+1} = 2u_n^2 - u_n - 1$. The first term is 0.

    a Find the 6th term of this sequence.

    b Jon says that if the first term of this sequence is 1, the 6th term will be less than 50. Is Jon right?

PB
ES
7 The first term of a sequence is 2. The 2nd term of the sequence is 4. The 3rd term of the sequence is 10. The rule for the

sequence is $u_{n+1} = au_n + b$.

    a Work out the values of a and b.

    b Which is the first term that is greater than 100?

PB
ES
8 Alan buys a car for £X. The value of the car depreciates by r% each year. After two years the value of the car is £12 800. After four years the value of the car is £8192.

    a Work out
       i the value of X
       ii the value of r.

    b For how many years will Alan have the car before it is worth less than £5000?

PB
ES
9 The first term of a geometric progression is 4. The 4th term of this geometric progression is 62.5.

Work out the sum of the first five terms.

PB
ES
10 Jasmine breeds hamsters. At the start of 2010, she had 600 hamsters. At the end of each year the number of hamsters increases by 50%. At the end of each year she sells a third of her hamsters.

    a How many hamsters did Jasmine have at the start of 2015?

    b If she had sold a half of her hamsters at the end of each year
       i how many hamsters would she have at the start of 2015? (Round down to the nearest whole number of hamsters.)
       ii in what year would she have no hamsters left?

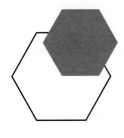

Algebra Strand 2 Sequences
Unit 8 nth term of a quadratic sequence

PS — PRACTISING SKILLS   **DF** — DEVELOPING FLUENCY   **PB** — PROBLEM SOLVING   **ES** — EXAM-STYLE

PS **1** Match each nth term formula to the correct quadratic sequence.

a $n^2 + 3n$ **A** 6, 8, 8, 6, 2

b $2n^2 - n - 5$ **B** 0, –1.5, –4, –7.5, –12

c $5n - n^2 + 2$ **C** –4, 1, 10, 23, 40

d $\dfrac{1 - n^2}{2}$ **D** 4, 10, 18, 28, 40

DF **ES** **2** The nth term of a sequence is given by $2n^2 - n - 1$.

a Write down the first five terms.

b Dulcie says that the even numbered terms are all odd numbers. Is Dulcie right?

PB **ES** **3** Bilal started a computer company in 2010. The profits of the company, in £ millions, for the first five years from 2010 were 0, 2, 6, 12, 20. If this pattern continues

a what profit might Bilal expect to make in the next year?

b what profit might Bilal expect to make after n years of the company's existence?

c in what year will the profits first exceed £100 million?

PB **ES** **4** The nth term of a sequence is given by $n^2 + an + b$. The 2nd term is –3 and the 4th term is 5.

a Work out the values of a and b.

b Paul says that the first term over 100 is 117.

  i Is Paul right? Show how Paul arrived at this answer.

  ii Write down the position of this term in the sequence.

PB **ES** **5** The nth term of a sequence is given by $n^2 + n + 1$.

a Kyle says that all the terms in this sequence are prime numbers. Show that Kyle is wrong.

b How many of the first ten terms are not prime numbers?

PB
ES
6 Here are the first three patterns in a sequence of patterns made from triangles and hexagons.

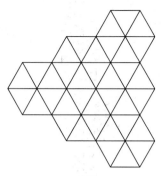

S is the sequence of the number of edges of the hexagons in each pattern. T is the sequence of the number of edges of the small triangles in each pattern.

The sequence formed by subtracting sequence T, term by term, from sequence S has an nth term given by $an^2 + bn$.

Work out the values of a and b.

PB
ES
7 The nth term of a sequence is given by $n^2 - 2n + 5$. The nth term of a different sequence is given by $n^2 + n - 7$.

a Which term has the same value and is in the same position in both sequences?

b Explain why this is the only common term.

PS
8 Work out the nth term of each of these quadratic sequences.

a 2, 2, 0, –4, –10

b –1, 0, 2, 5, 9

c –6, –4, 0, 6, 14

d –6, –4, 6, 24, 50

PB
ES
9 Bob and Laura work in a bird sanctuary. In the last three years, the numbers of a particular breed of bird have increased. The sequence below shows the number of birds each year.

20   40   80

Bob says that next year the number of these birds will be 140. Laura says that next year the number of these birds will be 160.

a Explain why both Bob and Laura may be right.

b How many of these birds will there be in five years' time

i if Bob is right?

ii if Laura is right?

10 Here are the first three patterns in a sequence of patterns
 made from sticks.

 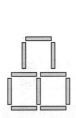 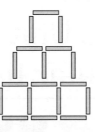

a Work out the number of sticks in the nth pattern.

b What is the greatest value of n that can be made with 200 sticks?

 11 The first five terms of a sequence are:

0   –1   –3   –6   –10

The nth term of the sequence is given by $\dfrac{n - n^2}{2}$.

a Find the 20th term.

b Is –100 a term in this sequence? Explain your answer.

 12 Here are the first five terms of a quadratic expression.

5   24   55   98   153

The nth term of this sequence is written in the form $an^2 + bn + c$.

a Work out the values of a, b and c.

b Prove that all the even numbered terms are even numbers.

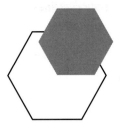

Algebra Strand 3 Functions and graphs Unit 8 Perpendicular lines

PS PRACTISING SKILLS   **DF** DEVELOPING FLUENCY   **PB** PROBLEM SOLVING   **ES** EXAM-STYLE

PS **1** Look at the diagram.

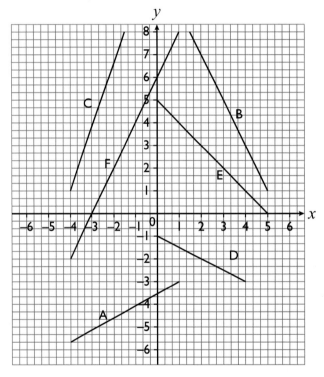

a Which of the lines on the grid are

 i parallel

 ii perpendicular

 to the line with equation $y = 2x - 3$?

b Write down an equation of each of the lines chosen in part **a**.

PS **ES** **2** Write down the gradient of a line perpendicular to the line with equation:

    a $y = 2x - 1$

    b $y = 1 - 2x$

    c $2y = 1 - x$

    d $x + 3y = 1$

    e $y - 1 = \dfrac{2x}{3}$

    f $5x + 4y = 20$

DF **ES** **3** ABC is a right-angled triangle. Angle A = 90°.

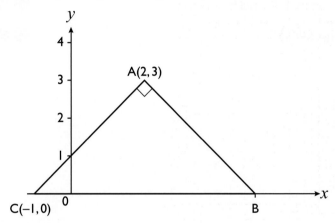

    a Write down an equation of the line AB.

    b Find the coordinates of B.

    c Work out the area of triangle ABC.

PS **ES** **4** Here are the equations of eight straight lines.

    A $y = 2x - 3$ **B** $y = 5 - 3x$ **C** $3y - x = 7$ **D** $x + y = 3$

    E $y = \dfrac{2x - 1}{2}$ **F** $y = 3(1 - x)$ **G** $y = \dfrac{x}{3} - 2$ **H** $x = 3(y + 2)$

    a Which lines are parallel?

    b Which lines are perpendicular to each other?

PB **ES** **5** Find an equation of a line perpendicular to $y = 4x + 3$ passing through the point $(1, 7)$.

PB
ES

6 a Draw the line with equation $2y = x - 2$. Use the same scale on each axis.

   b Find an equation of the line perpendicular to $2y = x - 2$ passing through (2, 0).

   c Work out the area of the triangle bounded by this perpendicular, the line $2y = x - 2$ and the y-axis.

PB
ES

7 a L is a line with equation $2x + 3y = 6$. On a grid, draw L.

   b The point (6, –2) lies on L. P is a straight line perpendicular to L passing through (6, –2). Find an equation for P.

   c Find the coordinates of the intercepts of P with the axes.

   d Find the area bounded by L, P and the x-axis.

PB
ES

8 AC is a diagonal of a kite ABCD.

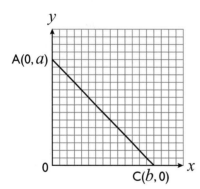

Prove that the equation of the other diagonal can be written as
$y = \dfrac{2bx + a^2 - b^2}{2a}$.

PB
ES

9 A(2, 2) and B(12, 2) are the end points of a diameter of a semicircle. The point P(4, 6) is a point on the circumference of the semicircle. Find the equation of the tangent to the semicircle at P.

PB
ES

10 ABCD is a square. A(4, 6) lies on the line with equation $y = 0.5x + 4$. The perpendicular to $y = 0.5x + 4$ passing through A meets the x-axis at B. AB is one side of the square ABCD.

Find the coordinates of the points C and D.

Algebra Strand 3 Functions and graphs Unit 9 Inverse and composite functions

PS PRACTISING SKILLS   **DF** DEVELOPING FLUENCY   **PB** PROBLEM SOLVING   **ES** EXAM-STYLE

PS **1** This function machine shows $f(x) = x - 3$.

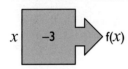

This function machine shows $g(x) = \dfrac{x}{10}$.

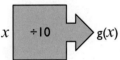

a Find
   i $f(7)$ **ii** $g(7)$.

b Find
   i $g(f(8))$ **ii** $f(g(8))$.

c Find
   i $f(f(10))$ **ii** $g(g(10))$.

PS **2** This function machine shows $f(x) = 5x$.

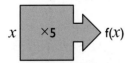

This function machine shows $g(x) = 2x - 3$.

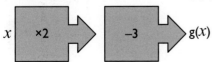

a Find

i $f^{-1}(x)$ ii $g^{-1}(x)$.

b Find

i $f^{-1}(30)$ ii $g^{-1}(7)$.

c Find

i $f^{-1}g(4)$ ii $g^{-1}f(4)$.

d Find

i $f^{-1}g^{-1}(11)$ ii $g^{-1}f^{-1}(8)$.

PB
ES
3 Here are two functions: $p(x) = 6x, q(x) = x + 5$.   ● ● ●

a Find

i $p(5)$ ii $q(-3)$.

b Show that $pq(x) \neq qp(x)$.

c Find

i $p^{-1}(x)$ ii $q^{-1}(x)$.

d Does $pp^{-1}(x) = qq^{-1}(x)$?

PB
ES
4 Here are two functions: $f(x) = x^2, g(x) = x + 2$.   ● ● ●

a Find $fg(8)$.

b Find $gf(7)$.

c For what value of x are $fg(x)$ and $gf(x)$ equal?

DF
ES
5 Here are two functions: $p(x) = 2x + 3, q(x) = 3x^2$.

a Find

i $p(-5)$ ii $q(4)$.

b Find $pq(2)$.

c Find $qp(2)$.

d Find

i $p^{-1}(x)$ ii $q^{-1}(x)$.

e Find $qp^{-1}(-2)$.

PB
ES
6 $f(x) = x^2, g(x) = x - 1, h(x) = 2x$ ● ● ●

a Find $fgh(2)$.

b Find $fgh(x)$.

c Jamie says $f(g + h)(x) = fg(x) + fh(x)$. Is Jamie right?

PB **ES** **7** Three functions are defined as $f(x) = x^2$, $g(x) = 3x - 1$ and $h(x) = 2x$.

    a Using **all three functions**, find the composite function that gives the largest value when $x = 3$.

    b Write down an expression for this function in terms of x.

PB **ES** **8** $f(x) = x + 1$, $fg(x) = 3x + 5$, $gh(x) = 3x^2 + 1$

    a Find

        i $g(x)$ **ii** $h(x)$.

    b Find $fgh(x)$.

    c Show that $hgf(x)$ can be written as $(ax + b)(x + 2)$.

DF **9** $f(x) = 5x + 2$, $g(x) = 3x - 7$, $h(x) = 2x$

    Find

    a $fg(x)$ **b** $gf(x)$ **c** $f^{-1}(x)$

    d $g^{-1}(x)$ **e** $(fg)^{-1}(x)$ **f** $(gf)^{-1}(x)$

    g $g^{-1}f^{-1}(x)$ **h** $f^{-1}g^{-1}(x)$.

    i Comment on your answers to **e**, **f**, **g** and **h**.

PB **ES** **10** $f^{-1}(x) = 3x - 2$, $g^{-1}(x) = \sqrt{x} + 1$, $x \geqslant 1$

    a Solve $f(x) = f^{-1}(x)$.

    b Find the positive value of x for which $f(x) - g(x) = 0$.

Algebra Strand 3 Functions and graphs Unit 10 Exponential functions

PS PRACTISING SKILLS   **DF** DEVELOPING FLUENCY   **PB** PROBLEM SOLVING   **ES** EXAM-STYLE

PS
ES
1 This is a table of values for $y = 1.5^x$.

x	-2	-1	0	1	2	3	4
y	0.44		1		2.25		

a Work out the missing values in this table of values.

b Draw a grid with x values from –2 to 4 and y values from –1 to 8. Draw the graph of $y = 1.5^x$.

c Use your graph to estimate the value of x for which $1.5^x = 3$.

PS
ES
2 This is a table of values for $y = 100 \times 4^{-x}$.

x	-2	-1	0	1	2	3	4
y	1600			25		1.5625	

a Work out the missing values in this table of values.

b Draw a sketch of the graph of $y = 100 \times 4^{-x}$ showing the value of the y-intercept, which is at the point P.

PS
ES
3 A curve has equation $y = a^x$ where a is a positive constant.

a Write down the coordinates of the point where this curve crosses the y-axis.

b The curve passes through the point with coordinates (3, 15.625). Work out the value of a.

c Work out the value of y when
  i $x = 0$
  ii $x = 2$.

PB
ES
4 Riaz invests £2000 into a bank account paying compound interest
at a rate of 3% per year. Irfan invests £2500 into a different bank
account paying compound interest at a rate of 1.5% per year.

The amount of money, £y, in a bank account after x years is given
by the formula $y = P \times a^x$ where £P is the amount of money invested
and a is a multiplication factor.

a Show that for Riaz's investment, $y = 2000 \times 1.03^x$.

b Find the formula for Irfan's investment.

c By drawing graphs of each formula, find an estimate for the value of x
for which the values of both investments are the same. Give your answer
to the nearest whole number.

DF
ES
5 The points $(1, 10)$ and $(4, 80)$ lie on the curve with equation $y = ab^x$,
where a and b are integers. If the points $(3, q)$ and $(p, 200)$ lie on the
curve, find the values of q and p.

PB
ES
6 A rubber ball is dropped from a height of x metres. Each time
the ball strikes the floor it rebounds to $\frac{4}{5}$ of the height it has just fallen.

a If the ball is dropped from a height of 15 metres, what distance will it
have travelled when it hits the floor for the 4th time?

b Write down an expression, in terms of x and n, for the height of the
ball after n bounces.

c Brian says the ball will carry on bouncing forever. Explain why Brian
is wrong.

DF
ES
7 The diagram shows a sketch of a curve with equation $y = pq^x$ where
p and q are constants.

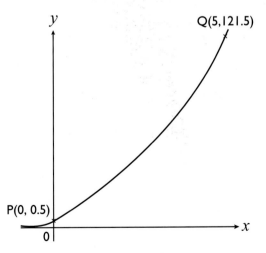

a Find the values of p and q.

b Find the value of r if $(-4, r)$ is a point on this curve.

PB
ES
8 A population of a certain species of bird is decreasing by 25% every year. At the start of 2010, the population of this species of bird was estimated at 2 million.

   a What was the population at the end of 2015?

   b If P is the population after x years, write down a formula for P in terms of x.

   c Estimate the year in which this species of bird is likely to become extinct.

PB
ES
9 Haider borrows £15 000 to buy a car. Each year, Haider repays 15% of the money that he still owes.

   a How much does Haider owe after

   i 4 years?

   ii n years?

   b As soon as Haider owes no more than £500, he pays off the remaining amount. How many years will it take Haider to repay what he owes?

PB
ES
10 In 1985, Emily bought a painting for £4500. The value of the painting increased by 20% each year. In 1990, Jason bought a painting for £15 000. The value of Jason's painting increased by 12% each year.

£V is the value of a painting after n years.

   a Write down an equation for V, in terms of n, for each of these two paintings.

   b In what year was Emily's painting first worth more than Jason's painting?

   c In what year did the value of Emily's painting exceed £1 million?

Algebra Strand 3 Functions and graphs Unit 11 Trigonometric functions

PS PRACTISING SKILLS   DF DEVELOPING FLUENCY   PB PROBLEM SOLVING   ES EXAM-STYLE

DF **1** This is a table of values for $y = \sin x$.

x	0°	15°	30°	45°	60°	75°	90°
y	0		0.5				1.0

a Work out the missing values in this table of values.

b On a suitable grid, draw the graph of $y = \sin x$ for values of x from 0° to 90°.

c Use this table to find

   i $\sin 120°$

   ii $\sin 135°$

   iii $\sin 210°$

   iv $\sin 330°$

   v $\sin 195°$

   vi $\sin 105°$

   vii $\sin 315°$

   viii $\sin 285°$

PS **2** $\sin x = 0.5$

Which of the following are also equal to 0.5?

a $\sin 150°$ **b** $\cos 30°$ **c** $\cos 150°$ **d** $\cos 60°$ **e** $\sin 210°$

f $\tan 150°$ **g** $\sin 390°$ **h** $\cos 300°$ **i** $\tan 30°$ **j** $\sin 330°$

DF
ES
3 The diagram shows the graphs of two trigonometric functions, $y = \sin x$ and $y = \cos x$.

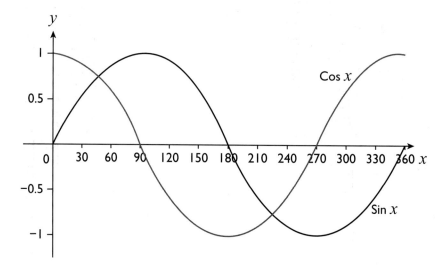

a Which is the graph of each function?

b For what values of x between 0° and 360° does $\sin x = \cos x$?

c Work out the difference between $\sin x$ and $\cos x$ when $x = 150°$.

DF **4** Write down

a the minimum value of y and

b the maximum value of y when

   i $y = \sin x$

   ii $y = \tan x$

   iii $y = \cos x$

   iv $y = \sin 2x$

   v $y = 2\sin x$

   vi $y = 5\sin 100x$

   vii $y = \dfrac{1}{2}\cos 2x$

   viii $y = 1 + \cos 4x$

   ix $y = \sin 5x + 3$

   x $y = 3 - 2\sin x$

PB **ES** **5** The London Eye is a tourist attraction where visitors sit in passenger cars on the outer edge of a giant revolving wheel.

The highest point on the London Eye is about 130 metres above the ground. The centre is about 70 metres above the ground.

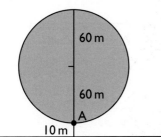

The London Eye starts to rotate at a time $t = 0$ minutes when A is at its lowest point. The distance, y metres, of A above the ground after t minutes is given by the equation $y = a + b \sin wt$ where a, b and w are integers.

If it takes 30 minutes for the point A to reach its highest point, find the values of a, b and w.

PB **ES** **6** The distance, y metres, of a particle from a given point O after t seconds is given by the formula $y = 6 + 4 \cos 10t$.

a Draw a graph of $y = 6 + 4 \cos 10t$ from $t = 0$ to $t = 18$ in steps of three seconds.

b For how many seconds is the particle more than five metres away from O?

c Find an estimate for the distance of the particle from O after five seconds.

DF **7** Here are sketches of the graphs of five functions.

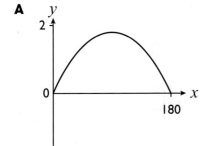

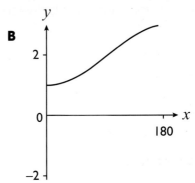

C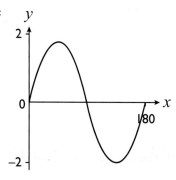

D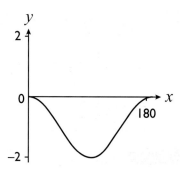

E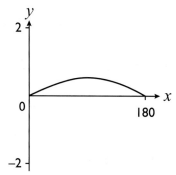

Match each of these functions with one of the graphs A to E.

i $y = \sin 2x$ **ii** $y = 2\sin x$ **iii** $2\sin 2x$ **iv** $y = \sin \dfrac{x}{2}$ **v** $y = \cos 2x - 1$

DF **ES** **8 a** Write down all the values of x between 0° and 360° for which $\cos x = -0.5$.

b Solve $1 + 2\cos 5x = 0$ for values of x between 0° and 90°.

PB **ES** **9 a** On 2 mm graph paper, draw graphs of the functions $y = \tan x$ and $y = \cos 2x$ for values of x between −180° and +180°.

b Use your graph to find an estimate to the solution of $\tan x = \cos 2x$ when 0° < x < 90°.

Algebra Strand 3 Functions and graphs Unit 12 The equation of a circle

PS — PRACTISING SKILLS   **DF** — DEVELOPING FLUENCY   **PB** — PROBLEM SOLVING   **ES** — EXAM-STYLE

PS **1** **a** Write down the co-ordinates of all points on the circle $x^2 + y^2 = 16$ which cross either the x-axis or the y-axis.

b Which of the points below lie on the circumference of the circle $x^2 + y^2 = 16$?

   i $(3, \sqrt{7})$ **ii** $(3, 5)$ **iii** $(2\sqrt{3}, 2)$ **iv** $(\sqrt{6}, 2\sqrt{5})$ **v** $(-2, 2\sqrt{3})$

   vi $(-\sqrt{7}, 3)$ **vii** $(-3, 5)$ **viii** $(-4, 0)$ **ix** $(2\sqrt{2}, -2\sqrt{2})$ **x** $(1, -\sqrt{5})$

PB **ES** **2** The circle $x^2 + y^2 = 36$ crosses the positive y-axis at A and the positive x-axis at B. C is the point $(8, 6)$.

Work out the area of triangle ABC.

PS **3** **a** Write down the equation of a circle of radius 5 units, centre the point $(0, 0)$.

b Find the radius of the circle with equation $x^2 + y^2 = 10$.

c A circle, centre the point $(0, 0)$, passes through the points $(a, 0)$ and $(0, a)$. Write down an equation of this circle.

PB **4** The diagram shows the graph of $x^2 + y^2 = 4$. AB is a diameter of the circle. A is the point with co-ordinates $(1, \sqrt{3})$.

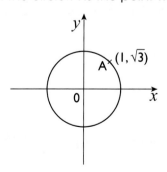

a Find the co-ordinates of B.

b Find the gradient of AB.

c Find an equation of the diameter AB.

d Find the equation of the tangent through B.

DF **5** Which of these straight lines are tangents to the circle with equation $x^2 + y^2 = 25$?

a $y = x - 5$ **b** $x = 5$ **c** $x + y = 5$ **d** $y = -5$

e $x = 5y$ **f** $x = -5$ **g** $y = 5x$ **h** $y = x + 5$

PB **ES** **6** The diagram shows the graph of $x^2 + y^2 = 9$. A, B, C and D are the vertices of a square which lie on the circle $x^2 + y^2 = 9$. A is the point with co-ordinates $\left(\sqrt{\dfrac{3}{2}}, \sqrt{\dfrac{3}{2}} \right)$.

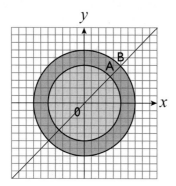

a Find the area of ABCD.

b Find the equation of the tangent at A.

PB **ES** **7** The diagram shows circles with equations $x^2 + y^2 = 25$ and $x^2 + y^2 = 49$.

a Find the co-ordinates of the points, A and B, where the line $y = x$ crosses the circles.

b Find the co-ordinates of the points where the tangent at A to $x^2 + y^2 = 25$ crosses $x^2 + y^2 = 49$, to the nearest integer.

PB **ES** **8** Kirsty says, 'The tangent to the circle $x^2 + y^2 = 25$ at the point $(3, 4)$ passes through the point $(5, 2.5)$.'

Is Kirsty right?

PB
ES

9 The diagram shows the graph of $x^2 + y^2 = n^2$ and the line $y = n$.
The point P(-3, b) lies on the circle $x^2 + y^2 = n^2$.

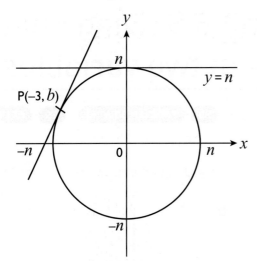

a Find an expression, in terms of n, for b.

b The tangent at P meets the line $y = n$ at (a, n). Show that
$$a = \frac{n\sqrt{n^2 - 9} - n^2}{3}.$$

PB
ES

10 The straight line with equation $x + y = 1$ intersects the circle with
equation $x^2 + y^2 = 4$ at the points A and B. C is the point with
co-ordinates $(-2, 0)$.

Find the area of triangle ABC.

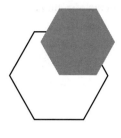

Algebra Strand 4 Algebraic methods Unit 6 Solving linear inequalities in two variables

 PRACTISING SKILLS   DEVELOPING FLUENCY   PB PROBLEM SOLVING    EXAM-STYLE

PS **1** Write down the inequality defined by the shaded region in each of these diagrams.

a

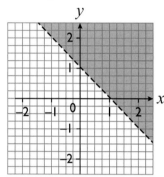

b

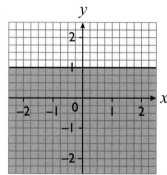

c

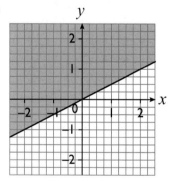

d

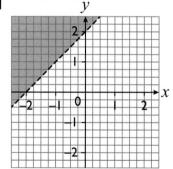

DF **2** Draw a diagram to show the region defined by the inequalities

ES $x + y \leq 4$ $\qquad$ $y < 3$ $\qquad$ $x \geq -1$ $\qquad$ $y > x$

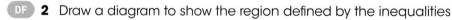

DF **3** **a** Write down the three inequalities which define this shaded region.

ES **b** Find the maximum value of $x + y$ in this region.

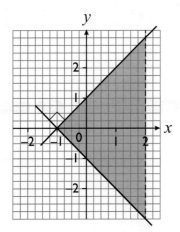

DF **4** A region A is defined by the inequalities $x + y \geqslant 3, x \leqslant 3$ and $y \leqslant x + 1$.

ES **a** Show this region on a diagram.

b The points (a, b) are points inside A, where a and b are integers.
Write down the co-ordinates of each of these points.

PB **5** Find the area, in square units, o.f the region defined by the inequalities

ES $2x + 3y \leqslant 6, y > x + 1$ and $x \geqslant -1$.

PB **6** Andy plays in a tennis tournament. The maximum number of matches

ES he can play is 16. Andy wins (W) at least three times as many matches
as he loses (L). He wins more than seven matches.

a Write down as many inequalities as you can in W and L.

b Show your inequalities on a diagram.

c If Andy gets 2 points for a win and 1 point for a loss, work out the least
number of points that he could get if he plays in just 10 matches.

PB **7** Jamil has a drawer containing 15 pairs of socks. He has more black

ES socks than white socks. The difference between the number of
black socks and the number of white socks is less than 12.

a Draw a diagram to show this information.

b Jamil's mum says that he has four pairs of white socks and nine pairs
of black socks in his drawer. Is she right?

PB
ES
8 Farmer Ted has some pigs and some chickens on his farm. The
shaded region on the diagram shows the possible numbers
of pigs, p, and chickens, c.

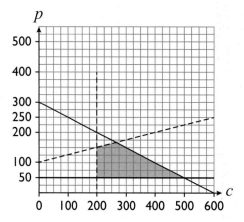

a Describe fully, in words, the relationships between the
number of pigs and the number of chickens on Ted's farm.

b The shaded region on the diagram shows the possible numbers of pigs
and chickens. Work out the greatest possible total number of pigs and
chickens on Ted's farm.

PB
ES
9 Pete is a property developer. He buys t terraced houses
and a apartments. Pete buys no more than eight properties.
He wants to have at least two more apartments than terraced houses.

a Write down four inequalities relating to t and a.

b Show these inequalities on a diagram.

c Each terraced house costs £120 000 and each apartment costs
£150 000. Work out the greatest amount of money that Pete will have
to spend.

Algebra Strand 4 Algebraic methods Unit 7 Solving equations numerically

PS — PRACTISING SKILLS   **DF** — DEVELOPING FLUENCY   **PB** — PROBLEM SOLVING   **ES** — EXAM-STYLE

DF ES 1 The equation $x^3 - 12x - 10 = 0$ has three solutions.

   a Jim says there is a solution between $x = 3$ and $x = 4$. Show that Jim is right.

   b Find this solution giving your answer correct to one decimal place.

DF ES 2 a Sketch the graph of $x^3 - 10x + 8 = 0$ for values of x from -5 to $+4$.

   b Find pairs of consecutive integers between which the solutions of $x^3 - 10x + 8 = 0$ lie.

   c Find the three solutions giving each answer correct to one decimal place.

DF ES 3 The equation $x^3 - 2x^2 - 4x - 3 = 0$ has just one solution. Find this solution giving your answer correct to one decimal place.

PS 4 Show that

   a the equation $x^3 - 5x^2 + 9 = 0$ can be written as $x = 5 - \dfrac{9}{x^2}$

   b the equation $x^3 + 7x - 2 = 0$ can be written as $x = \dfrac{2}{x^2 + 7}$

   c the equation $x^3 - 2x^2 - 45 = 0$ can be written as $x = \sqrt{2x + \dfrac{45}{x}}$.

PB ES 5 Here is a solid cone. The volume of the cone is $100\,\text{cm}^3$.

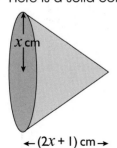

x cm

$\leftarrow (2x + 1)\,\text{cm} \rightarrow$

Find the area of the base of the cone correct to two decimal places.

45

DF **ES** **6 a** Use the iterative formula $x_{n+1} = \sqrt[3]{5x_n + 4}$ with $x_0 = 2.6$ to find x_1, x_2, x_3 and x_4.

   b What do the values of x_1, x_2, x_3 and x_4 show you?

DF **ES** **7 a** Show that the equation $x^2 - 5x - 3 = 0$ can be written as the iterative formula $x_{n+1} = \sqrt{5x + 3}$.

   b Taking $x_0 = 5$, find a solution of $x^2 - 5x - 3 = 0$ to one decimal place.

DF **ES** **8 a** Show that the equation $x^3 - 8x - 4 = 0$ has a solution between $x = 3$ and $x = 4$.

   b Write down an iterative formula that could be used to find this solution.

   c Find this solution giving your answer correct to two decimal places.

PB **ES** **9** Here is a cube A of side x cm and a cylinder B of radius x cm and height x cm. The difference between the number of cm³ in A and the number of cm² in the curved surface area of B is 10.

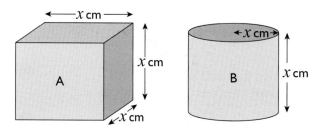

   a Use this information to find an equation in x.

   b Using an iterative process, or otherwise, find a possible value of x. Give your answer correct to two decimal places.

Algebra Strand 4 Algebraic methods Unit 8 Proving general results

PS — PRACTISING SKILLS   DF — DEVELOPING FLUENCY   PB — PROBLEM SOLVING   ES — EXAM-STYLE

PS **ES** **1 a** Show that the difference between two prime numbers is sometimes a prime number and sometimes not.

    b Find two prime numbers such that the sum of their squares is **not** an even number.

PB **ES** **2** Here is a triangle ABC. All angles are measured in degrees.

A

$2x + 30$

B $5x - 20$ $4x + 5$ C

    Prove that triangle ABC can never be an isosceles triangle.

PS **ES** **3 a** Prove that the product of three consecutive whole numbers is always an even number.

    b Prove that the sum of three consecutive odd numbers is always an odd number.

PS **ES** **4 a** Prove that the product of two odd numbers is always an odd number.

    b Prove that the difference between the squares of two consecutive odd numbers is always an even number.

    c What can you say about the sum of the squares of two consecutive odd numbers?

DF **ES** **5** n is a positive integer. When is each of the following expressions an even number: sometimes, always or never?

    i $2n - 1$ **ii** $n^2 - 1$ **iii** $(4n - 3)^2$ **iv** $n(n + 1)(n - 10)$ **v** $(2n + 7)(3n - 1)$

PB **ES** **6** $f(n) = n^2 - 4n - 21$

    John says that if $n \neq 0$, $f(n)$ is always an even number. Janet says that $f(n)$ is only an even number when n is an odd number. Who is right?

DF
ES
7 *n* and *a* are integers. Prove that $(n - a)^2 - (n + a)^2$ is always an even number divisible by 4.

PB
ES
8 Here is a triangle.

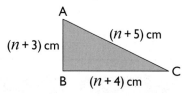

If $n \neq 0$, prove that triangle ABC is **not** a right-angled triangle.

PS
ES
9 a Show that $(x - 4)^2 - (x + 1)^2 = 5(3 - 2x)$.

b Show that $\dfrac{t^2 - 4}{t^2 + t - 2} = \dfrac{t - 2}{t - 1}$

c Show that $(n + 5)(n - 2)(n - 3) = n^3 - 19n + 30$.

DF
10 Show which of the following quadratic equations have real roots and which have no roots. Give a reason for your decision on each equation.

a $x^2 - 3x - 8 = 0$

b $x^2 - 3x + 8 = 0$

c $x^2 + 3x - 8 = 0$

d $x^2 + 3x + 8 = 0$

Algebra Strand 5 Working with quadratics Unit 3 Factorising harder quadratics

PS — PRACTISING SKILLS   DF — DEVELOPING FLUENCY   PB — PROBLEM SOLVING   ES — EXAM-STYLE

PS 1 Factorise these.

    a $6x^2 + 2x - 20$

    b $6x^2 - 22x + 20$

    c $6x^2 - 58x - 20$

    d $6x^2 - 26x + 20$

    e $6x^2 - 34x + 20$

    f $6x^2 - 26x - 20$

PS 2 Solve these.

    a $2x^2 + 5x - 3 = 0$

    b $3x^2 - 27 = 0$

    c $3x^2 + 5x = 2$

    d $(2x - 1)^2 = 3x^2 - 2$

PB **3** The diagram shows four identical rectangular tiles placed in
ES a pattern, surrounding a square. The area of each rectangle is $80\,cm^2$.

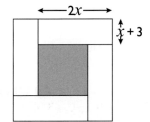

Find the area of the grey square.

DF **4** Factorise $4(x + 2)^2 - 8(x + 2) - 5$.
ES

DF **5** Simplify these.

  a $\dfrac{x^2 - 16}{2x^2 - 9x + 4}$

  b $\dfrac{x^3 - 9x^2 + 20x}{2x^3 - 6x^2 - 20x}$

  c $\dfrac{6x^2 - 2x}{2x^2 - 7x - 4} \div \dfrac{6x^2 + x - 1}{-2x^2 + 9x - 4}$

DF **6** Factorise these.

  a $6ac + bd + 3bc + 2ad$

  b $6a^3 - 12b^2 - 9ab + 8a^2b$

  c $x^4 - 1$

PB
ES **7** A man is four times as old as his son. Five years ago the product of their ages was 234.

  a If x is the age of the son, show that $4x^2 - 25x - 209 = 0$.

  b Solve $4x^2 - 25x - 209 = 0$ to find their present ages.

PB
ES **8** A stone is dropped down a well. The distance, in metres, the stone has fallen is given by the expression $6t + 5t^2$, where t is the time in seconds.

  How long does it take for the stone to reach a depth of 155 metres?

PB
ES **9** The diagram shows a picture inside a frame. The picture is in the shape of a rectangle, 10 cm by 8 cm. The width of the frame is x cm all round the picture. The grey area of the frame is 63 cm².

  a Show that $4x^2 + 36x - 63 = 0$.

  b Solve $4x^2 + 36x - 63 = 0$ and give the dimensions of the outside of the frame.

PB
ES **10** Here is a right-angled triangle.

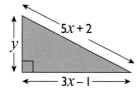

  $y = \sqrt{15}$

  If all measurements are in centimetres, work out the perimeter of the triangle.

Algebra Strand 5 Working with quadratics Unit 4 Completing the square

 PS — PRACTISING SKILLS    DF — DEVELOPING FLUENCY   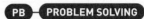 PB — PROBLEM SOLVING    ES — EXAM-STYLE

PS **1** Write these expressions in the form $(x + a)^2 + b$.

   a $x^2 + 6x$

   b $x^2 + 14x$

   c $x^2 - 40x$

   d $x^2 - 66x$

PS **2** Write these expressions in the form $(x + a)^2 + b$.

   a $x^2 + 2x - 5$

   b $x^2 + 8x + 3$

   c $x^2 - 10x - 1$

   d $x^2 - 5x - 3$

   e $x^2 + x + 6$

PS **3** Write these expressions in the form $p(x + q)^2 + r$.

   a $6x^2 - 24x + 7$

   b $2x^2 + 7x - 3$

   c $5x^2 - 90x + 14$

PB
ES **4** The height of a page in a book is 4 cm more than the width of the page. The area of the page is 132 cm².
   Find the height of the page.

PB
ES
5 The diagram shows a sketch of the graph of the function
$f(x) = (x - 4)^2 + 3$.
$P(0, c)$ is the intercept on the y-axis and $T(a, b)$ is the turning point of the graph.

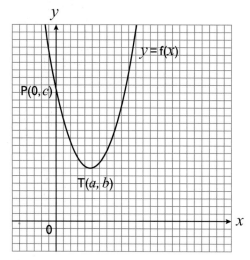

a Find the values of a, b and c.

b Write down an equation of $f(x - 2)$.

c Sketch the graph of $f(x - 2)$.

DF **6** Find the coordinates of

i the turning point, and

ii the y-intercept of the graph of each of these equations.

a $y = (x + 3)^2 - 4$

b $y = x^2 - 10x + 3$

c $y = x^2 - x - 5$

d $y = 2x^2 - 8x + 11$

PB
ES
7 The diagram shows a right-angled triangle.
$y^2 = p(x + q)^2 + r$

a Find the values of p, q and r.

b **i** Find the minimum value of $p(x + q)^2 + r$.

ii Explain why y^2 can't have this value.

c Find the actual minimum value of y^2.

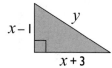

PB
ES

8 The diagram shows a square and a right-angled triangle.
All measurements are in centimetres. The areas of the square
and the right-angled triangle are the same.

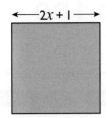
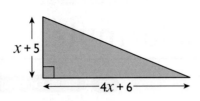

$2x + 1$

$x + 5$

$4x + 6$

Find the perimeter of the square.

PB
ES

9 A lawn measures 12 metres by 8 metres. It is surrounded by a flower
bed of area $52\,\text{m}^2$ as shown in the diagram. The flower bed is of
equal width around the lawn.

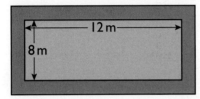

12 m

8 m

Find the width of the flower bed.

PB
ES

10 Ian throws a cricket ball in the air. The equation of the height,
h metres, reached by the ball is $h = 12t - 4.9t^2$ where t is the time,
in seconds.

a By completing the square, find the greatest height reached by
the ball.

b Work out the time taken to reach this height.

Algebra Strand 5 Working with quadratics Unit 5 The quadratic formula

PS — PRACTISING SKILLS   DF — DEVELOPING FLUENCY   PB — PROBLEM SOLVING   ES — EXAM-STYLE

PS 1 $ax^2 + bx + c = 0$ is the general form of a quadratic equation.
Write down the values of a, b and c for these equations.

   a $x^2 + 3x - 7 = 0$

   b $5x^2 - x + 20 = 0$

   c $5 - 2x - x^2 = 0$

   d $x^2 = 5x + 4$

   e $5(x - 2x^2) = 9$

PS 2 i For each of the quadratic equations in Question 1, state whether
$b^2 - 4ac < 0$, $b^2 - 4ac = 0$ or $b^2 - 4ac > 0$.

   ii What can be said about the roots of a quadratic equation when
$b^2 - 4ac < 0$, $b^2 - 4ac = 0$ or $b^2 - 4ac > 0$?

DF 3 Solve each of the quadratic equations in Question 1.

PB ES 4 An open box has dimensions 5 cm by x cm by $(x + 1.5)$ cm.
The surface area of the box is 37 cm².

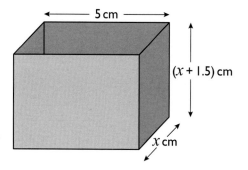

Work out the value of x.

PB **ES** **5** The diagram shows a right-angled triangle. All measurements are in centimetres.

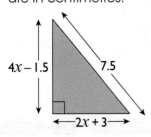

$4x - 1.5$ 7.5

$\longleftarrow 2x + 3 \longrightarrow$

Work out the area of this triangle.

DF **6** Solve these.

a $\dfrac{3}{x} = \dfrac{x-7}{5}$

b $\dfrac{2m+3}{m} = \dfrac{1-m}{5}$

c $\dfrac{n+5}{2n} = \dfrac{n-4}{9}$

d $(4w - 3)(3w + 2) = (5w + 2)(2w + 1)$

PB **ES** **7** The diagram represents a circular path surrounding a circular pond. The width of the path is 2 metres. The area of the path is a half of the area of the pond. The average depth of the pond is 1.5 metres.

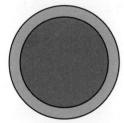

Work out the volume of water in the pond.

PB **ES** **8** Sam walks a distance of 15 km at an average speed of v km/h. Jane walks the same distance of 15 km at an average speed of 2 km/h faster than Sam. Jane takes 90 minutes less than Sam.

Work out Sam's average speed.

PB **ES** **9** The diagram shows a trapezium.

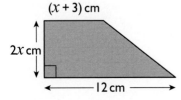

$(x + 3)$ cm

$2x$ cm

$\longleftarrow$ 12 cm $\longrightarrow$

Work out the perimeter of the trapezium if its area is 30 cm².

PB **10** **a** *n* is an integer. The sum of *n* and its reciprocal is also an integer. Find *n*.

ES

b *p* is an integer. The sum of *p* and its reciprocal is 2.5. Find *p*.

c The sum of a number and its reciprocal is 6. What possible number could this be?

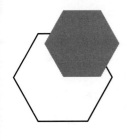

Algebra Strand 5 Working with quadratics Unit 6 Simultaneous equations with quadratics

PS – PRACTISING SKILLS   DF – DEVELOPING FLUENCY   PB – PROBLEM SOLVING   ES – EXAM-STYLE

PS **1** The curve $y = x^2 - 4x + 7$ and the line $y = 3x - 2$ intersect in two places. ●●●
Which of these equations when solved gives the x-coordinates of the points of intersection?

    a $x^2 - x + 5 = 0$ **b** $x^2 - 7x + 5 = 0$ **c** $x^2 + 7x - 5 = 0$

    d $x^2 - 7x + 9 = 0$ **e** $x^2 + x + 9 = 0$

PS
ES **2** The diagram shows the graph of the equation $y = x^2 - 5x + 3$. ●●●
The lines L, M and N each cross the graph of $y = x^2 - 5x + 3$ at two points.

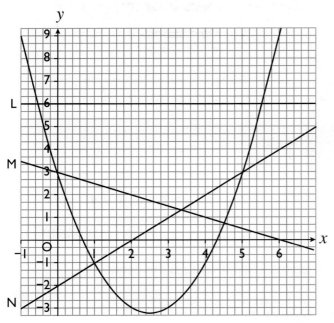

Write down which line gives the roots of each of these quadratic equations.

    a $2x^2 - 9x = 0$ **b** $x^2 - 5x - 3 = 0$ **c** $x^2 - 6x + 5 = 0$

    d $x^2 - 5x + 3 = 0$

PS **3** For each of these pairs of equations

    i write down the number of points of intersection of the line and the curve

    ii find the coordinates of any points of intersection.

    a $y = x^2 + 5$ and $y = 2$ **b** $y = x^2 - 4x$ and $y = 3 - 2x$

    c $y = 4x^2 - 10x + 5$ and $y = 2x - 4$ **d** $x^2 + y^2 = 10$ and $x + y = 5$

DF **4** Solve these simultaneous equations.

ES
    a $y = 2x^2$ and $y + 2x = 4$

    b $y = 2x^2 - 4x - 1$ and $2y + x = 0$

PB **5 a** Work out the missing values in this table of values for $y = x^2 + x - 2$.

ES

x	-3	-2	-1	0	1	2	3
y		0		-2			10

    b Draw the graph of $y = x^2 + x - 2$.

    c Use your graph to estimate solutions of the equation $x^2 - x - 5 = 0$.

PB **6** The diagram shows the graph of $x^2 + y^2 = 25$. L is a straight line with

ES   equation $y = 2x - 3$.

Find the coordinates of the points where L crosses the circle.

DF **7** The straight line with equation $y = ax + b$ is a tangent to the

ES   curve $y = x^2 - 4x + 7$ at the point $(1, 4)$.

    Find the value of a and the value of b.

DF **ES** **8** **a** Solve the simultaneous equations $y = x^2 - 4x - 1$ and $y + x = 3$.

b Sketch a graph of the curve $y = x^2 - 4x - 1$ and the line $y + x = 3$.

c Interpret your answer to **a** in terms of the graph.

PB **ES** **9** The straight line $x + y = 2$ is a tangent to the circle $x^2 + y^2 = 2$ at the point (p, q).

a Find the value of p and the value of q.

b The line $x + y = 1$ crosses the circle at A and B. Find the coordinates of A and B.

Algebra Strand 5 Working with quadratics Unit 7 Solving quadratic inequalities

PS – PRACTISING SKILLS   **DF** – DEVELOPING FLUENCY   **PB** – PROBLEM SOLVING   **ES** – EXAM-STYLE

PS **1** Solve these inequalities.

  a $(x - 2)(x + 5) > 0$

  b $(x - 2)(x + 5) \leq 0$

  c $(2x - 1)(x - 4) \geq 0$

  d $(2x - 1)(x - 4) < 0$

  e $x^2 - 3x \leq -2$

PS **2** The diagram shows the graph of the equation $y = x^2 - 5x$.

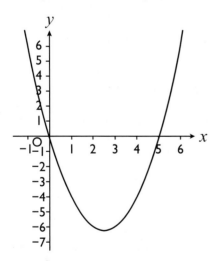

Use the graph to solve these.

  a $x^2 - 5x < 0$

  b $x^2 - 5x \geq 0$

  c $x^2 - 5x + 4 \leq 0$

  d $x^2 - 5x + 4 > 0$

  e $x^2 - 5x - 6 < 0$

  f $x^2 - 5x - 6 \geq 0$

PS **3** n is an integer between −8 and +8. Write down all the values of n that satisfy these inequalities.

    a $n^2 - n - 6 < 0$ **b** $n^2 - n < 0$ **c** $n^2 + n - 42 \geqslant 0$

    d $n^2 - 7n - 30 < 0$ **e** $6n^2 + n - 40 \leqslant 0$

DF **4** **a** Solve the equation $10 + 3x - x^2 = 0$.

ES   **b** Sketch the graph of $y = 10 + 3x - x^2$.

    c Write down the inequality defined by the closed region between the graph and the x-axis.

DF **5** **a** Sketch the graph of $y = 2x^2 + 5x - 3$.

ES   **b** On your sketch show the region where $2x^2 + 5x - 3 \leqslant 0$ and $y < x$.

PS **6** n is an integer. Write down all the values of n that satisfy these.

    a $n^2 < 9$ and $n^2 - 3n - 10 > 0$

    b $n^2 - 4n - 5 \leqslant 0$ and $n^2 + n - 12 \geqslant 0$

PB **7** Denzil is laying a rectangular base for a garage. The width of the base is w metres. The length of the base must be 2 metres less than three times the width. The area of the base must not be greater than $21\,\text{m}^2$.

ES

    a Write down an expression, in terms of w, for the area of the base.

    b Write down an inequality for this area.

    c Solve your inequality to give a range of possible values of w.

PB **8** Peter kicks a ball down a slope. The distance, s metres, travelled by the ball after t seconds is given by the formula $s = 20t + 2t^2$. Brian must stop the ball before it has travelled 112 metres.

ES

    a Write down an inequality in terms of t to show this information.

    b Solve your inequality to find the greatest amount of time that Brian has to stop the ball.

DF **9** $\dfrac{x(x-5)}{(x-2)(x+3)} > 0$

ES

    a What inequalities must $x(x - 5)$ and $(x - 2)(x + 3)$ both satisfy for this to be true?

    b For each of your inequalities in **a**, write down the possible range of values for x.

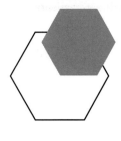

Algebra Strand 6 Properties of non-linear graphs Unit 1 Using chords and tangents

PS — **PRACTISING SKILLS**   **DF** — **DEVELOPING FLUENCY**   **PB** — **PROBLEM SOLVING**   **ES** — **EXAM-STYLE**

PS **1** Work out the gradient of a line joining

    a $(5, 6)$ and $(8, 12)$

    b $(0, 4)$ and $(-3, 9)$

    c $(-1, -5)$ and $(-6, 3)$

    d $(-2, 0)$ and $(-9, -4)$.

PS **2** The graphs of the curves $y = x^2 - x - 4$ and $y = 2x^2 + 3x - 1$ cross at points A and B.

Work out the gradient of AB.

DF
ES **3** Here is the graph of $y = 2x - x^2$.

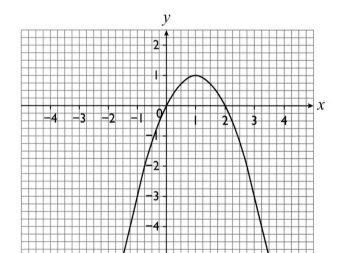

    a At what point on the graph is the gradient of the tangent equal to 0?

    b Find the gradient of the tangent to the curve at the point where $x = 0.5$.

    c Find the gradient of the chord from $(0, 0)$ to $(3, -3)$.

DF **ES** **4** Car A accelerates from 0 mph to 60 mph in five seconds.
Car B accelerates from 0 mph to 60 mph in eight seconds.
Here is the velocity–time graph for each car.

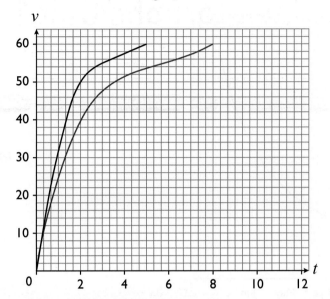

a Which curve represents each car?

b What is the difference between the accelerations of the two cars after three seconds?

c Find the average acceleration of each car during the first two seconds.

PB **ES** **5** A frozen pizza is taken out of a freezer to defrost. The graph shows the increase in temperature, P °C, after a time of t hours.

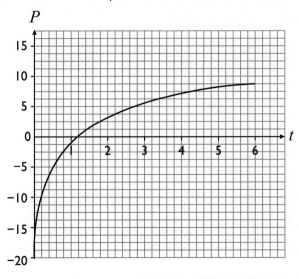

a Estimate the temperature of the pizza when it was taken out of the freezer.

b After what time was the rate of increase in temperature at its greatest?

c Estimate the rate of increase in temperature after one hour.

PB
ES

6 The graph shows the increase in temperature, $T\,°C$, during the first six months of 2015.

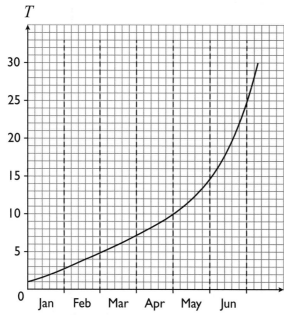

a Work out the average rate of increase in temperature per month.

b Estimate the rate of increase of temperature per month on 30th April.

PB
ES

7 A block of plastic and a block of iron are heated to a temperature of 60°C. The graph shows the cooling curve for each block.

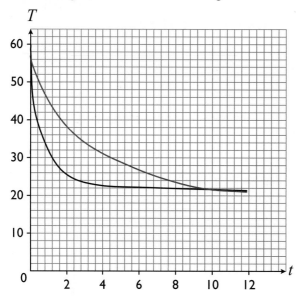

a Which curve represents the cooling of each block?

b Work out the average rate of cooling in the first five minutes for each block.

c Compare the rates of cooling of the two blocks after one minute.

PB
ES
8 Ishmal is at a garage, filling the petrol tank in his car with petrol. The graph shows the amount of petrol, L litres, in the petrol tank after t seconds.

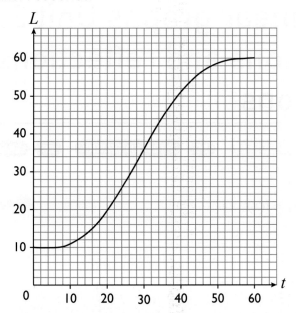

a Work out the average rate at which the tank was filled.

b After how many seconds was the rate of flow of petrol the same as the average rate?

c Explain why the graph is not a straight line.

PB
ES
9 The table of values shows the population of a rare breed of bird during the last eight years.

Year	1	2	3	4	5	6	7	8
Population (in 1000s)	15	9	6	3	2	1.7	1.5	1.0

a Draw a graph to show the decrease in population of this breed of bird.

b Find an estimate for the rate of decrease after three years.

A bird sanctuary is developing strategies to increase the population. They predict a population of 5000 birds in the next four years.

c Continue your graph to show this predicted increase.

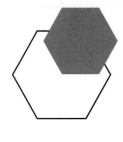

Algebra Strand 6 Properties of non-linear graphs Unit 2 Translations and reflections of functions

PS — PRACTISING SKILLS   DF — DEVELOPING FLUENCY   PB — PROBLEM SOLVING   ES — EXAM-STYLE

PS **1** Here is the graph of a function $y = f(x)$.

ES

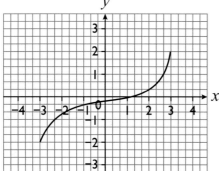

Match each of these functions with one of the graphs A to D.

a $y = f(x - 1)$ **b** $y = f(x + 1)$ **c** $y = f(x) - 1$ **d** $y = f(x) + 1$

A

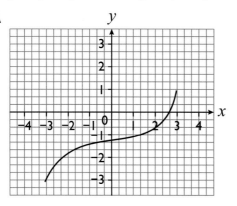

B

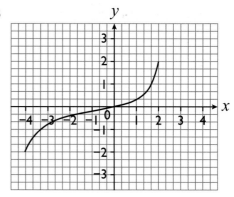

C

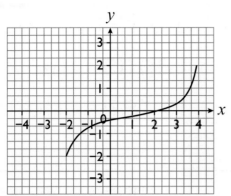

D

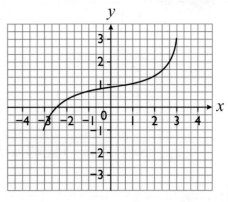

DF
ES

2 a Find the missing numbers in this table of values for the functions $f(x) = x^2$, $f(x - 1)$ and $f(x + 1)$.

x	-3	-2	-1	0	1	2	3
$f(x) = x^2$	9	4	1	0	1	4	9
$f(x - 1)$							
$f(x + 1)$							

b Sketch graphs of $y = f(x - 1)$ and $y = f(x + 1)$.

c Describe the single transformation from $y = f(x - 1)$ to $y = f(x + 1)$.

DF
ES

3 Here is the graph of a function $y = g(x)$.

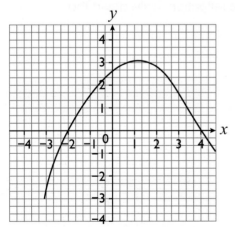

a On the same axes, draw the graphs of

i $y = g(-x)$

ii $y = -g(x)$.

b Write down the coordinates of the points where the graphs of

i $y = g(-x)$, and

ii $y = -g(x)$ cross the x- and y-axes.

DF **4** Here is the graph of $y = \sin x$.

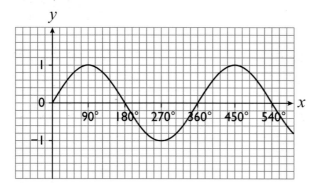

a Draw a sketch of a translation of the graph of $y = \sin x$ by the vector $\begin{pmatrix} 90° \\ 0 \end{pmatrix}$.

b Which of the following equations describes the translated graph in **a**?

i $y = \sin x + 90°$ **ii** $y = \sin(x + 90°)$ **iii** $y = \sin(x - 90°)$

iv $y = \sin x - 90°$ **v** $y = -\sin x$

DF **5** $f(x) = 2x + 1$

a Draw the graph of $y = f(x)$.

b **i** On the same axes, draw the reflection of $y = f(x)$ in the y-axis.

     ii $y = f(ax + b)$ is the equation of this reflection. Write down the values of a and b.

c Draw the graph of $y = f(x - 3)$ on your axes.

PB
ES
6 Here is the graph of a function $y = g(x)$. Write down the co-ordinates of

    a the turning point, and

    b the intercept on the x-axis of the graph of each of the following functions.

       i $y = g(x - p)$ **ii** $y = 2g(x)$ **iii** $y = -g(x) + 5$

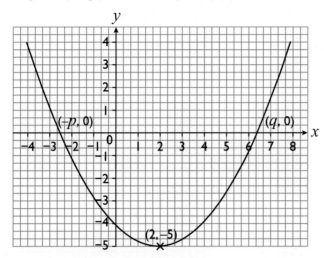

PB
ES
7 Here is the graph of a function $y = f(x)$.

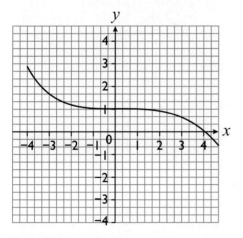

Transformation A:

The curve $y = f(x)$ is reflected in the x-axis and then translated by the vector $\begin{pmatrix} 0 \\ -2 \end{pmatrix}$.

Transformation B:

The curve $y = f(x)$ is translated by the vector $\begin{pmatrix} 0 \\ -2 \end{pmatrix}$ and then reflected in the x-axis.

Josh says that transformation A is identical to transformation B.

Is Josh right? Explain your answer with diagrams.

PS **8** Here is the graph of a function $y = f(x)$.

ES

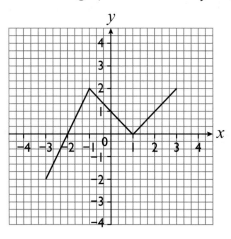

Match each of these functions with one of the graphs A to D.

a $y = f(2x)$ **b** $y = f\left(\dfrac{1}{2}x\right)$ **c** $y = 2f(x)$ **d** $y = \dfrac{1}{2}f(x)$

A

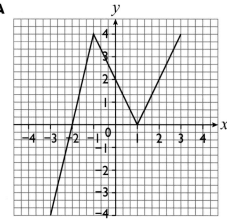

B

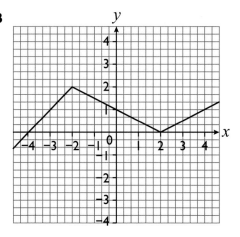

C

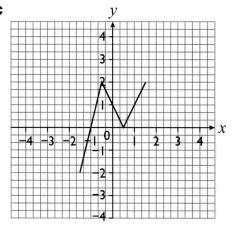

D

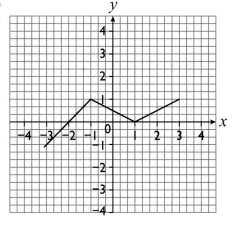

Algebra Strand 6 Properties of non-linear graphs Unit 3 Area under non-linear graphs

PS PRACTISING SKILLS   DF DEVELOPING FLUENCY   PB PROBLEM SOLVING   ES EXAM-STYLE

PS **ES** **1** Find the area of A, B, C and D and hence find the area between the curve and the x-axis.

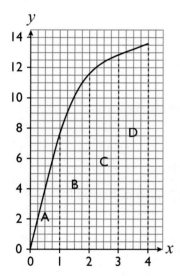

PS **ES** **2** Here is the graph of $y = x^2 - 2x + 2$, from $x = 0$ to $x = 4$.

Estimate the area under the curve and above the x-axis between $x = 0$ and $x = 4$ by finding the sum of the areas of four strips of equal width.

PS **3** Here is the graph of the function $y = 1 + 2^x$.

ES

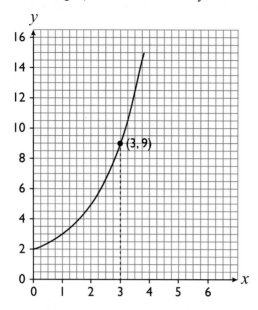

a Estimate the area under the graph and above the x-axis from $x = 0$ to $x = 3$ by

i counting squares, and

ii splitting the area into three strips of equal width.

b Which method do you think is the more accurate? Give a reason for your answer.

PB **4** The speed of a boat is taken at 10-second intervals for one minute. The table of values shows this information.

ES

Time in seconds	0	10	20	30	40	50	60
Speed in km/h	0	4	12	24	40	45	45

a Draw a velocity–time graph to show these results.

b Estimate the distance travelled by the boat in 60 seconds.

PB **ES** **5** Here are the velocity–time graphs for two cars.

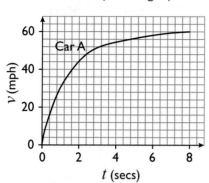 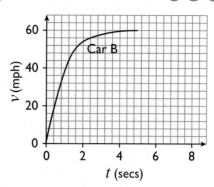

Work out the difference, in yards, between the distances it took the cars to reach 60 mph.

1 mile = 1760 yards

PB **ES** **6** The table shows the velocity of a rocket in the first three minutes after its launch.

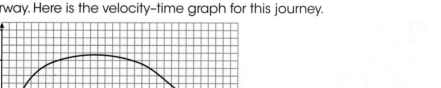

Time in minutes	0	0.5	1	1.5	2	2.5	3
Speed in km/min	0	10	30	150	360	800	1500

a Draw a velocity–time graph to show these results.

b Estimate the distance travelled by the rocket in the second minute of its flight.

PB **ES** **7** Harry drove his car between junction 2 and junction 3 on the M1 motorway. Here is the velocity–time graph for this journey.

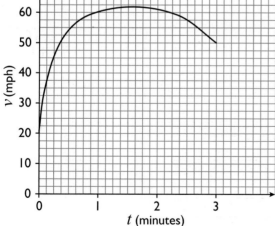

a How many minutes did it take Harry to drive between junction 2 and junction 3?

b Using three strips of equal width, work out an estimate for the distance, in miles, between junction 2 and junction 3.

c Is your estimate above or below the exact distance? Explain your answer.

73

PB
ES

8 The graph shows the decrease in the rate of cooling of a bowl of soup.

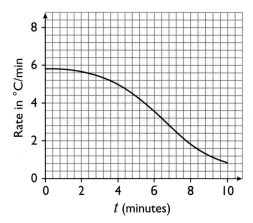

a Find an estimate for the area under this graph.

b What does this area represent?

Geometry and Measures Strand 2 Properties of shapes Unit 11 Circle theorems

PS — PRACTISING SKILLS   **DF** — DEVELOPING FLUENCY   **PB** — PROBLEM SOLVING   **ES** — EXAM-STYLE

PS **1** Find the size of the angle marked with a letter in each diagram. Give a reason for each of your answers.

a

b

c

PS **2** Each circle in this question has a centre O. Find the size of the angle marked with a letter. Give a reason for each of your answers.

a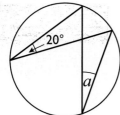

b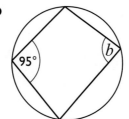

c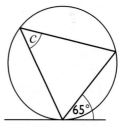

DF **ES** **3** The diagram shows a circle centre O. PA and PB are tangents to the circle.

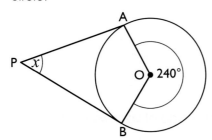

Find the size of the angle marked x.

75

PB
ES
4 P, Q, R and S are points on the circumference of a circle centre O.
Angle PRQ = 50°.

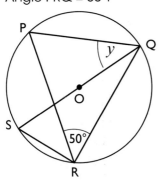

Find the size of the angle marked y. Give reasons for each stage of your working.

DF
ES
5 D, E and F are points on the circumference of a circle centre O. Angle
DOF = 140°.

Work out the size of the angle marked g. Give reasons for each stage of your working.

PB
ES
6 TP and TR are tangents to the circle centre O.

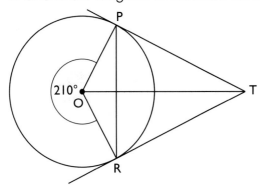

Find the size of angle PTR. Give reasons for each stage of your working.

PB **ES** **7** A, B and C are points on the circle centre O. Angle ABC is $x°$.
TA and TC are tangents to the circle.

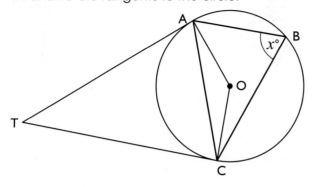

Prove that TA = TC.

PB **ES** **8** B, C, D and E are points on the circumference of the circle centre O.
EB is parallel to DC. XD is a tangent to the circle at D.

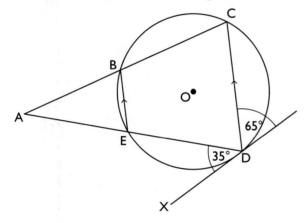

Using the information on the diagram prove that triangle ABE is isosceles.

PB **ES** **9** AB, BC and CA are tangents to the circle at P, Q and R respectively.
Angle B = $2x°$. Angle C = $2y°$.

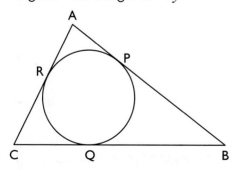

Find an expression in terms of x and y for the size of angle PQR.

PB **ES** **10** The circle centre O has a radius of 7 cm. The circle centre P has a radius of 10 cm. AB is a tangent to both circles.

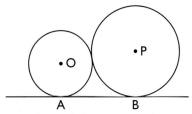

a Find the length of AB.

b What assumptions have you made in your solution?

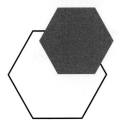

Geometry and Measures
Strand 3 Measuring shapes
Unit 7 The cosine rule

PS PRACTISING SKILLS   **DF** DEVELOPING FLUENCY   **PB** PROBLEM SOLVING   **ES** EXAM-STYLE

PS **1** Calculate the length of the marked with a letter in each side of these triangles. Give your answers correct to three significant figures.

a

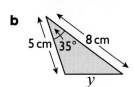

b

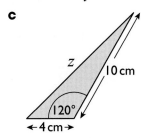

c

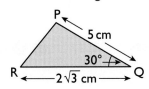

PS **2** PQR is a triangle.

ES

Work out the length of the side PR. Give your answer in surd form.

PS **3** Calculate the size of the angles marked with a letter in these diagrams.
Give your answers correct to one decimal place.

a

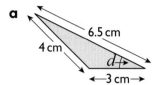

b

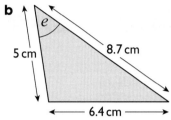

c

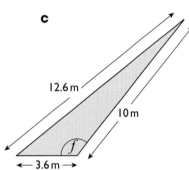

DF **4** Ipswich is 20 miles due east of Sudbury. Colchester is
ES 18.5 miles on a bearing of 230° from Ipswich.

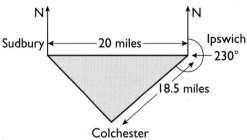

Find the distance of Sudbury from Colchester.

DF **5** The perimeter of this isosceles triangle is 25 cm. The shortest
ES side QR is 7 cm.

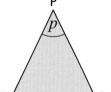

Find the size of angle p.

DF **ES** **6** Here is triangle ABC. Angle A is 40°. $b = 9.8$ cm, $c = 7.2$ cm. Find the length of BC.

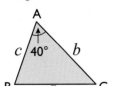

PB **ES** **7** A boat delivers supplies to two oil rigs. The boat sails from the harbour, H. It sails in a straight line from H to R, then from R to S then back to H. The bearing of R from H is 050°. The bearing of S from H is 120°. R is 20 km from H. S is 15 km from H.

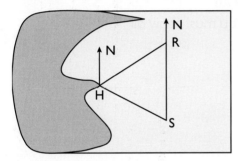

Work out the total distance the boat travels. Give your answer correct to one decimal place.

PS **ES** **8** A surveyor measures a farmer's field and puts the measurements on this sketch.

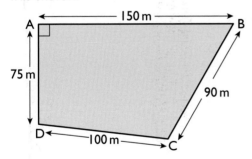

Find the size of angle BCD. Give your answer correct to one decimal place.

PB
ES

9 A builder ropes off the outline of a triangular plot of ground.
PQ = 45 m, PR = 60 m and angle QPR = 75°.

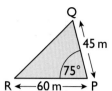

What is the shortest length of rope the builder needs? Give your answer to the nearest metre.

PB
ES

10 The diagram shows the roof of a house. There needs to be at least 2 m from the top of the roof at C to the base of the roof AB.

Does this roof meet these requirements? You must show all your working.

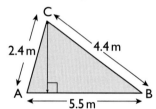

Geometry and Measures
Strand 3 Measuring shapes
Unit 8 The sine rule

PS — PRACTISING SKILLS   DF — DEVELOPING FLUENCY   PB — PROBLEM SOLVING   ES — EXAM-STYLE

PS **1** Calculate the length of the side marked with a letter in each
of these triangles. Give your answers correct to three significant figures.

a

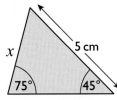

b

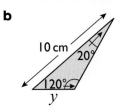

c

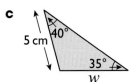

PS **2** PQR is a triangle.

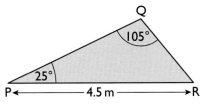

Work out the length of the side PQ. Give your answer correct to two
decimal places.

PS **3** Calculate the size of the angles marked with a letter in these diagrams. ●●●
Give your answers correct to one decimal place.

a

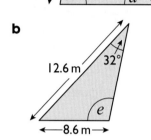

b

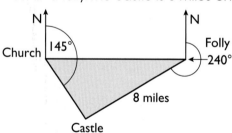

c

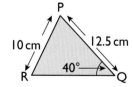

DF
ES **4** A castle is on a bearing of 145° from a church. The church is due ●●●
west of a folly. The castle is 8 miles on a bearing of 240° from the folly.

N
Church 145°
N
Folly
-240°
8 miles
Castle

Find the distance of the folly from the church.

DF
ES **5** In triangle PQR, PQ = 12.5 cm, Angle Q = 40° and PR = 10 cm. ●●●

P
10 cm
12.5 cm
40°
R   Q

Find two possible values for the size of angle R.

PS ES **6** Here is triangle ABC. Angle A is 40°. b = 9.8 cm, c = 7.2 cm.
Find the area of the triangle ABC.

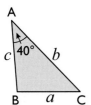

DF ES **7** Triangle XYZ has an area of 40 cm². XY = 10 cm, XZ = 12 cm.
Find the size of angle X.

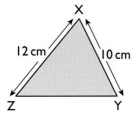

PB ES **8** A surveyor measures a farmer's field and puts the measurements
on this sketch.

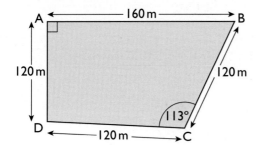

Find the area of the field. Give your answer correct to three significant
figures.

PB ES **9** Rob is planning an orienteering trip. He is going to walk from P to
Q to R and then back to P. Q is on a bearing of 050° from P.
R is on a bearing of 160° from Q and 110° from P. PQ = 7.5 km.

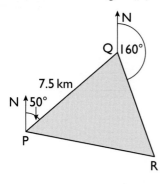

How far is Rob planning to walk? Give your answer correct to three
significant figures.

PB
ES

10 The diagram shows the cross section of a large tent. There needs
to be at least 3.5 m from the top of the tent at C to the base of the tent AB.

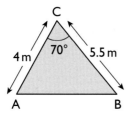

Does this tent meet these requirements? You must show all
your working.

Geometry and Measures
Strand 5 Transformations
Unit 11 Combining transformations

PS — PRACTISING SKILLS   DF — DEVELOPING FLUENCY   PB — PROBLEM SOLVING   ES — EXAM-STYLE

PS
ES

1 Triangle P is drawn on a coordinate grid. Triangle P is reflected in the line $x = 0$ and then reflected in the line $y = 1$ to give triangle Q.

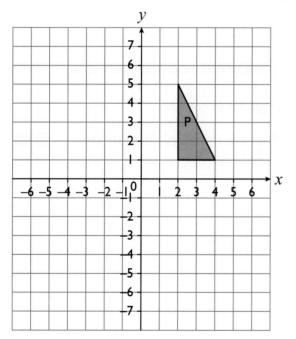

a Describe fully the single transformation which maps triangle P onto triangle Q.

b Name any invariant point in this single transformation.

PS **ES** **2** Triangle T is drawn on a coordinate grid. Triangle T is reflected in the y-axis. It is then reflected in the line $y = x$ to give triangle R.

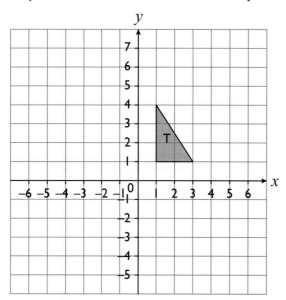

a Describe fully the single transformation which maps triangle T onto triangle R.

b Name any invariant point in this single transformation.

DF **ES** **3** The triangle A is enlarged with scale factor 2, centre (0, 0), to shape B. Shape B is then rotated 180° about (0, 2) to shape C.

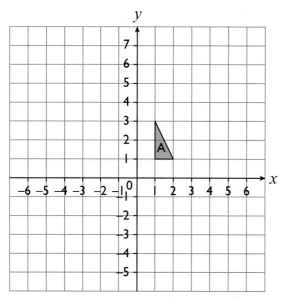

a Describe fully the single transformation which maps triangle A back onto triangle C.

b Name any invariant point in the single transformation.

PB **4** Look at the diagram.

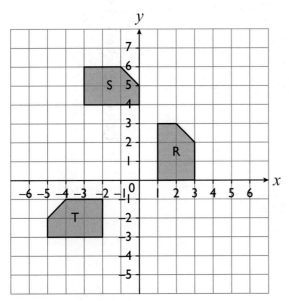

a **i** Describe the single transformation that maps R onto S.

ii List any invariant points in this transformation.

iii Describe a combination of transformations that maps R onto S.

b **i** Describe the single transformation that maps R onto T.

ii List any invariant points in this transformation.

iii Describe a combination of transformations that maps R onto S.

PB
ES **5** A shape S is drawn on a coordinate grid. The shape is reflected in the line $x = a$. It is then reflected in the line $y = b$.

Describe the single transformation that can replace these two reflections.

PB
ES **6** A shape T is drawn on a coordinate grid. The shape is reflected in the line $x = a$. It is then reflected in the line $x = b$.

Describe the single transformation that can replace these two reflections.

7 The shape P is rotated 90° anticlockwise about (0, 2) followed by 180°
 about (−1, 1) onto shape Q.

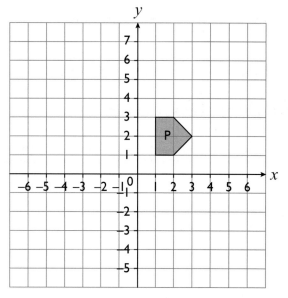

a Describe fully the single transformation which maps shape P onto shape Q.

b Name any invariant point in the single transformation.

Geometry and Measures
Strand 5 Transformations
Unit 12 Enlargement with negative scale factors

PS ─ PRACTISING SKILLS   DF ─ DEVELOPING FLUENCY   PB ─ PROBLEM SOLVING   ES ─ EXAM-STYLE

PS
ES
1 Triangle A is drawn on a coordinate grid. Describe fully the single transformation which maps triangle A onto triangle B.

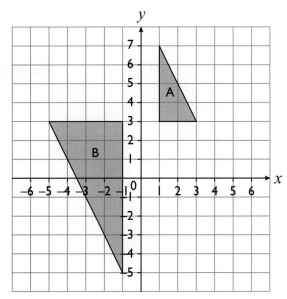

PS
ES **2** Triangle C is drawn on a coordinate grid. Describe fully the single transformation which maps triangle C onto triangle D.

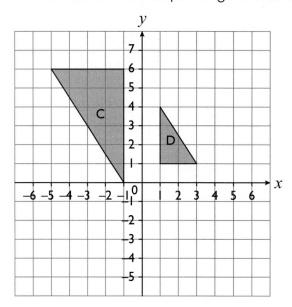

DF
ES **3** Enlarge triangle A with

   a scale factor −2, centre (0, 0)

   b scale factor −½, centre (−2, 1).

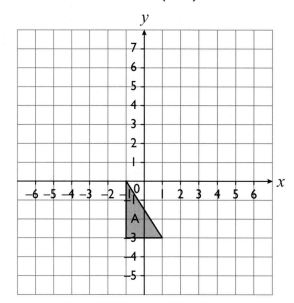

DF **4** Look at the diagram.

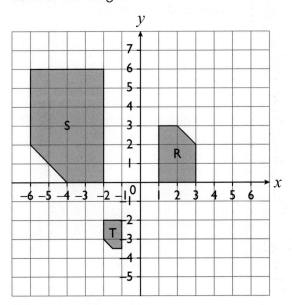

a Describe the single transformation that maps R onto S.

b Describe the single transformation that maps R onto T.

PB **5** A shape, F, is drawn on a coordinate grid. The shape is rotated 180°
ES about the origin.

Describe a different single transformation that can replace this rotation.

PB **6** A shape G is drawn on a coordinate grid. The shape is reflected
ES in the line $x = a$. It is then reflected in the line $y = b$.

Describe two different single transformations that can replace these
two reflections.

7 The shape P is enlarged with scale factor –3, centre (0, 0), to shape Q.
The shape Q is enlarged with scale factor –½, centre (0, 3), to shape R.

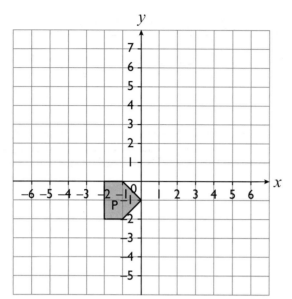

a Draw these enlargements on a coordinate grid.

b Write down the single transformation that takes P directly to R.

Geometry and Measures
Strand 5 Transformations
Unit 13 Trigonometry in 2-D and 3-D

PS — PRACTISING SKILLS   **DF** — DEVELOPING FLUENCY   **PB** — PROBLEM SOLVING   **ES** — EXAM-STYLE

PS
ES
1 Here is a cuboid. The cuboid has length 12 cm, width 5 cm and height 6 cm.

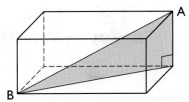

a Work out the length of the diagonal AB.

b Work out the angle AB makes with the base of the cuboid.

PB
ES
2 A stirrer used to stir paint sticks 10 cm out of a paint tin. The tin of paint is 30 cm tall and is a cylinder of radius 8 cm.

a Work out the length of the stirrer.

b What angle does the stirrer make with the base of the tin?

DF
ES
3 Here is a cuboid. It has a length of 12 cm, a width of 6 cm and a height of 4 cm. The vertices of the grey triangle are on the midpoints of three of the edges of the cuboid.

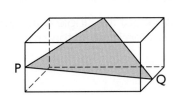

a Work out the perimeter of the grey triangle.

b Work out the angle that PQ makes with the base of the cuboid.

PB **ES** **4** David wants to fit a long stick into a box which is in the
shape of a cuboid. The length of the box is 0.9 m, the width
is 30 cm and the height is 30 m.

    a What is the longest stick that will fit into the box?

    b What is the angle the longest stick will make with the base of
the box?

PB **ES** **5** Here is a sketch of a grain silo. The grain silo is
made from a cylinder and a cone of radius 3 m.
The height of the cylinder is 8 m.
The height of the cone is 4 m.

    Work out the size of the obtuse angle that the
edge of the cone makes with the edge of
the cylinder.

DF **6** Here is a diagram of a cold frame.
The cold frame is in the shape of
a right-angled triangular prism.
A straight piece of metal joins P to Q
to strengthen the frame.

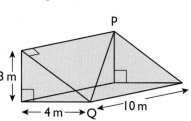
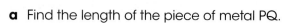
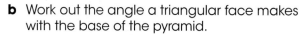

    a Find the length of the piece of metal PQ.

    b Find the angle that PQ makes with the base of the cold frame.

DF **7** Here is a pyramid. It has a square base of side 10 cm and
a vertical height of 12 cm.

    a Work out the angle the edge of a triangular
face makes with the base of the pyramid.

    b Work out the angle a triangular face makes
with the base of the pyramid.

8
 Here is a cuboid. The length is 15 cm. The width is 8 cm.
The height is 6 cm.

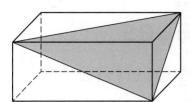

Work out the area of the grey triangle.

 9 Raj is running a TV cable across his bedroom. The cable follows the
black line on the diagram. The room is 4 m long, 3 m wide and 2.5 m high.

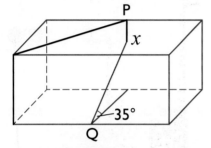

P is halfway along the length of one wall. Q is halfway along another wall.
X is the point where the TV is to be placed. Raj wants the angle that
XQ makes with the floor of the room to be 35°.

Work out the length of TV cable Raj needs. You must show all
your working.

10 Here is the plan of design for the roof of a conservatory. The roof
is in the shape of an octagonal pyramid. The base of the roof is
a regular octagon of side 1 m. The height of the roof is 0.6 m. The
angle each face makes with the base of the roof has to be more
than 30°.

Does this design match the requirements? You must show how you
reach your conclusion.

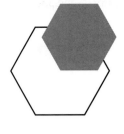

Geometry and Measures
Strand 6 3-D shapes
Unit 8 Area and volume in similar shapes

PS — PRACTISING SKILLS   DF — DEVELOPING FLUENCY   PB — PROBLEM SOLVING   ES — EXAM-STYLE

PS 1 Two spheres have diameters in the ratio 3:5.

    a Work out the ratio of their surface areas.

    b Work out the ratio of their volumes.

PS 2 The grey cylinder has been enlarged by a linear scale factor of 1.5 from the white cylinder.

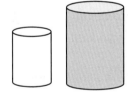

    a Write down the ratio of their radii.

    b Work out the ratio of their surface areas.

    c Work out the ratio of their volumes.

PS 3 Here are two similar children's building bricks. The grey brick is a linear enlargement of the white brick by scale factor 2. The volume of the white brick is 20 cm³.

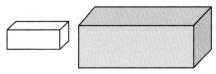

Work out the volume of the grey brick.

DF
ES
4 Here are two similar bottles of water. The small bottle holds one litre of water. The ratio of the heights of the bottles is 2:3.

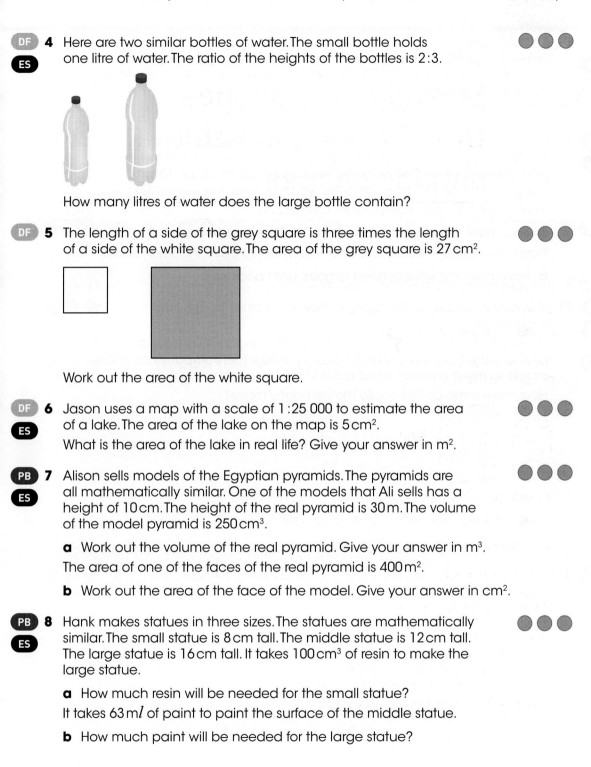

How many litres of water does the large bottle contain?

DF
5 The length of a side of the grey square is three times the length of a side of the white square. The area of the grey square is $27\,cm^2$.

Work out the area of the white square.

DF
ES
6 Jason uses a map with a scale of 1:25 000 to estimate the area of a lake. The area of the lake on the map is $5\,cm^2$.
What is the area of the lake in real life? Give your answer in m^2.

PB
ES
7 Alison sells models of the Egyptian pyramids. The pyramids are all mathematically similar. One of the models that Ali sells has a height of 10 cm. The height of the real pyramid is 30 m. The volume of the model pyramid is $250\,cm^3$.

a Work out the volume of the real pyramid. Give your answer in m^3.
The area of one of the faces of the real pyramid is $400\,m^2$.

b Work out the area of the face of the model. Give your answer in cm^2.

PB
ES
8 Hank makes statues in three sizes. The statues are mathematically similar. The small statue is 8 cm tall. The middle statue is 12 cm tall. The large statue is 16 cm tall. It takes $100\,cm^3$ of resin to make the large statue.

a How much resin will be needed for the small statue?
It takes 63 m*l* of paint to paint the surface of the middle statue.

b How much paint will be needed for the large statue?

99

PB 9
ES

Phillipe makes models of the Eiffel Tower that are mathematically similar. The small model has a height of 10 cm. The large model has a height of 15 cm. It takes 120 g of metal to make the small model. Phillipe has 360 g of metal.

Does he have enough metal to make a large model?

PB 10
ES

Fiona is making solid podiums of two sizes for an awards ceremony. The two podiums will be mathematically similar. The height of the small podium will be 9 cm. The height of the large podium will be 15 cm.

The podiums are going to be made from concrete. The materials to make the concrete for the large podium cost £62.50

a How much will the materials cost to make the small podium?

Fiona calculated it would take one tin of paint to paint the small podium.

b How many tins will she need to paint both podiums?

PB 11
ES

A company makes plastic bottles. They make small bottles and large bottles.

The small bottles have a height of 10 cm. The large bottles have a height of 25 cm. The bottles are mathematically similar. The company has enough plastic to make a million small bottles.

How many large bottles could the company make?

Geometry and Measures
Strand 7 Vectors Unit 2
Proofs with vectors

PS — PRACTISING SKILLS   **DF** — DEVELOPING FLUENCY   **PB** — PROBLEM SOLVING   **ES** — EXAM-STYLE

PS   **1**   M is the midpoint of PQ. Find, in terms of **p** and/or **q**

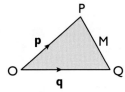

   a $\overrightarrow{QP}$

   b $\overrightarrow{OM}$.

PS   **2**   ABCD is a parallelogram.

ES $\overrightarrow{AB} = \mathbf{a}$ $\overrightarrow{BC} = \mathbf{b}$

   P is the point on CD such that CP:PD = 2:3.

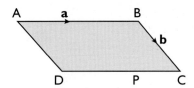

   a   Find $\overrightarrow{CP}$.

   b   Prove that $\overrightarrow{AP} = \mathbf{b} + \dfrac{3}{5}\mathbf{a}$.

PS   **3**   M is the midpoint of PQ. N is the point on OM so that ON:NM = 2:1.

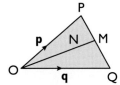

Write $\overrightarrow{ON}$ in terms of **p** and **q**.

PS **ES** **4** PQRS is a rectangle.

$\overrightarrow{PQ} = \mathbf{p}$ $\overrightarrow{QR} = \mathbf{q}$

M is the midpoint of PS.

NS = SR

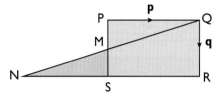

a Find $\overrightarrow{QM}$.

b Prove that QMN is a straight line.

DF **ES** **5** WXYZ is a parallelogram. P is the midpoint of WX. Q is the midpoint of PY. R divides XY in the ratio XR:RY = 2:1.

$\overrightarrow{WX} = 2\mathbf{d}$ $\overrightarrow{XY} = 3\mathbf{e}$

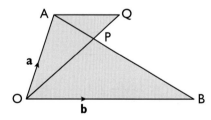

Prove that W, Q and R are collinear.

PB **ES** **6** $\overrightarrow{OA} = \mathbf{a}$ $\overrightarrow{OB} = \mathbf{b}$

4AP = AB

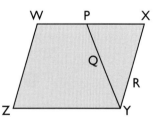

If $\overrightarrow{AQ} = k\mathbf{b}$, find the value of k.

PB **ES** **7** $OP:OX = 3:4$

$OQ:OY = 3:4$

$\overrightarrow{OX} = 4\mathbf{x}$ $\overrightarrow{OY} = 4\mathbf{y}$

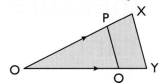

Prove that PQ is parallel to XY and $PQ = \frac{3}{4}XY$.

PB **ES** **8** ABC is a triangle. CDP is a straight line.

The point Q divides BC so that $BQ:QC = 3:1$.

The point D divides CP so that $CD:DP = 2:3$ and $AD:DB = 1:2$.

$\overrightarrow{CQ} = \mathbf{q}$ $\overrightarrow{CP} = \mathbf{p}$

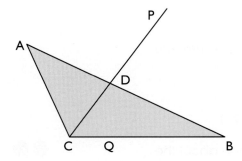

Prove that $\overrightarrow{AC} = 2\mathbf{a} - \frac{3}{5}$.

PB **9** The points O, A, B, not in the same straight line, are such that $\overrightarrow{OA} = \mathbf{a}$, $\overrightarrow{OB} = \mathbf{b}$. Points C and D are such that $\overrightarrow{OC} = 4\mathbf{a}$ and $\overrightarrow{OD} = 4\mathbf{b}$.

a Express $\overrightarrow{AD}$ and $\overrightarrow{BC}$ in terms of $\mathbf{a}$ and $\mathbf{b}$.

P is the point on AD such that $AP = \frac{1}{5}AD$.

b Express $\overrightarrow{AP}$, $\overrightarrow{OP}$ and $\overrightarrow{BP}$ in terms of $\mathbf{a}$ and $\mathbf{b}$, and show that P divides BC in the ratio $1:4$.

Given also that the figure OCED is a parallelogram,

c express $\overrightarrow{OE}$ in terms of $\mathbf{a}$ and $\mathbf{b}$.

d State in words what this result shows about

   i the points O, P and E

   ii the lengths of OP and OE.

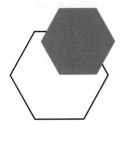

Statistics and Probability
Strand 1 Statistical measures
Unit 5 Interquartile range

PS **1** For each of these data sets, find

   i the median

   ii the interquartile range.

   a 4, 6, 9, 11, 17, 18, 25

   b 13.5, 15.7, 16.1, 16.8, 16.9, 17.1, 17.5

   c 1, 4, 9, 16, 25, 36, 49, 64, 81, 100, 121, 144, 169, 196, 225

   d −8, −5, −3, −2, −2, 0, 3, 5, 7, 8, 10

   e 12, 16, 15, 11, 7, 10, 9

   f 3.6, 2.7, 4.8, 1.6, 8.3, 7.9, 6.8, 5.4, 3.3, 5.7, 7.0

PS **2** The stem and leaf diagram gives information about the
number of books sold by a shop on each day in January last year.

2	5	5	6	7	8	8	9		
3	0	3	4	5	5	7	7	7	8	9
4	1	1	2	2	3	5	5	6	7	9
5	3	5	7	7					

Key: 2 | 5 represents 25 books

Find

   a the median

   b the interquartile range of the data.

PS **3** The box plot gives information about the lengths, in mm, of some worms.

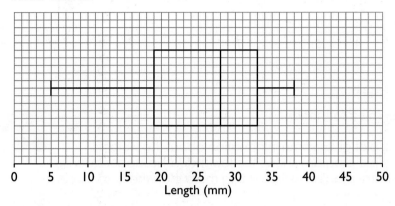

Find

a the median length

b the interquartile range of the lengths.

PS **4** The cumulative frequency diagram gives information about the weights, in grams, of 50 letters.

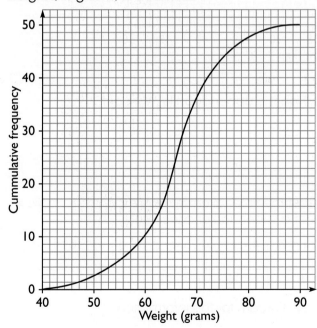

a Find an estimate for the median weight.

b Find an estimate of the interquartile range.

PS **5** The stem and leaf diagram gives information about the number of calls to a call centre on each of 15 days.

3	7	8	8	9	
4	0	3	4	5	6	7
5	0	1	2	2	3	

Key: 3 | 7 represents 37 calls

Draw a box plot for this information.

DF **6** The incomplete box plot gives some information about the weights, in kg, of some dogs. The diagram shows the lower quartile, upper quartile and highest weight. The median weight is 8 kg more than the lower quartile.

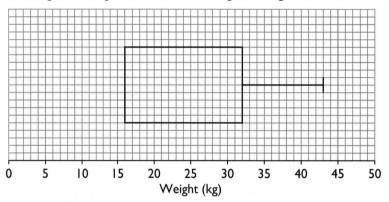

Weight (kg)

a Work out the median weight.

The lowest weight is 25 kg less than the upper quartile. Work out

b the lowest weight

c the range of the weights

d the interquartile range.

DF **7** The table gives information about the time taken, in minutes, to serve each of 80 customers at a supermarket check-out.

Time taken (t minutes)	$0 < t \leqslant 2$	$2 < t \leqslant 4$	$4 < t \leqslant 6$	$6 < t \leqslant 8$	$8 < t \leqslant 10$	$10 < t \leqslant 12$
Frequency	7	8	15	23	20	7

a Draw a cumulative frequency diagram for this information.

b Find an estimate for
  i the median time
  ii the interquartile range.

The shortest time taken to serve a customer was 0.5 minutes.

The longest time taken to serve a customer was 11 minutes.

c Draw a box plot for the distribution of the times taken to serve these customers.

8 The box plots show information about the average number of miles per gallon (mpg) achieved by a sample of cars in 1990 and in 2010.

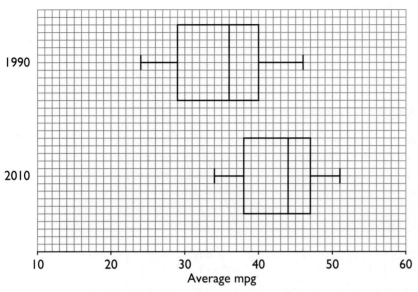

a Write down

  i   the highest average mpg in 1990

  ii the lowest average mpg in 2010.

b Compare the medians and the interquartile ranges of the average mpg of these cars.

9 The cumulative frequency diagram gives information about the times taken by some children to do a test. More girls took 50 minutes to do the test than boys.

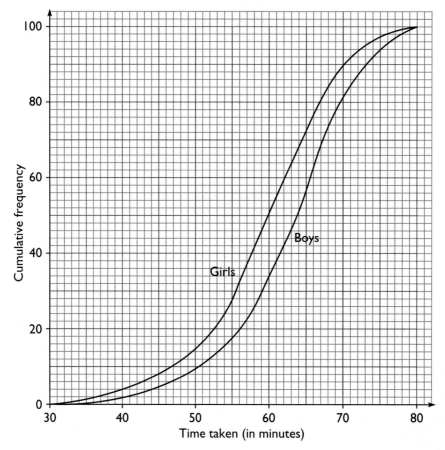

a Estimate how many more.

b Work out the percentage of boys who took more than 70 minutes to do the test.

c Compare the medians and the interquartile ranges of the times taken by these boys and girls to do the test.

10

Tony and Sarah each played a computer game 19 times.
Here are the scores they got in each game.

Tony

44	58	65	58	64	57	53	48	63	57
55	50	49	61	45	64	55	61	49	

Sarah

60	45	52	55	57	41	59	43	48	46
59	61	48	44	47	53	43	65	55	

a Draw an ordered back-to-back stem and leaf diagram for this
information. You must include a key.

Tony		Sarah
	4	
	5	
	6	

b Copy and complete the following table.

	Tony	Sarah
Lowest score	i	41
Lower quartile	49	ii
Median	iii	52
Upper quartile	iv	59
Highest score	65	v

c Draw box plots to show the scores for Tony and Sarah.

d Compare the scores of Tony and Sarah.

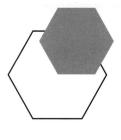

Statistics and Probability
Strand 2 Statistical diagrams
Unit 8 Histograms

PS – **PRACTISING SKILLS**   **DF** – **DEVELOPING FLUENCY**   **PB** – **PROBLEM SOLVING**   **ES** – **EXAM-STYLE**

PS **1** Here is a list of types of diagrams.

bar chart   **vertical line chart**   **frequency diagram**   **histogram**

Write down the diagram, or diagrams, from the list you would use to represent

a categorical data

b discrete data

c continuous data (equal class widths)

d continuous data (unequal class widths).

PS **2** Zach recorded the weights, in grams, of some mice. His results are summarised in the grouped frequency table.

Weight (w grams)	Frequency	Class width	Frequency density (frequency ÷ class width)
$5 < w \leqslant 10$	8	5	1.4
$10 < w \leqslant 15$	10	5	**i**
$15 < w \leqslant 20$	23	**ii**	**iii**
$20 < w \leqslant 25$	**v**	**iv**	3.4

a Find entries **i**, **ii**, **iii**, **iv** and **v** in the table.

b Draw a histogram to represent the data.

PS **3** James recorded the times, in minutes, it took him to travel to work.
The histogram shows information about his results.

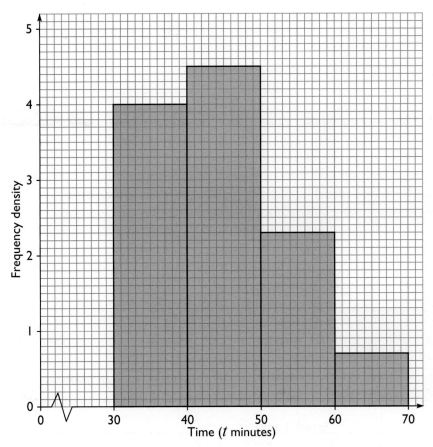

Use the information in the histogram to find **a**, **b**, **c**, **d**, **e** and **f** the table.

Time (t minutes)	Frequency density	Class width	Frequency (frequency density × class width)
$30 < t \leqslant 40$	4	10	40
$40 < t \leqslant 50$	**a**	10	**b**
$50 < t \leqslant 60$	2.3	**c**	**d**
$60 < t \leqslant 70$	**e**	**f**	**g**

PS **4** The histogram shows information about the speed of the water flowing in a river on each of 90 days.

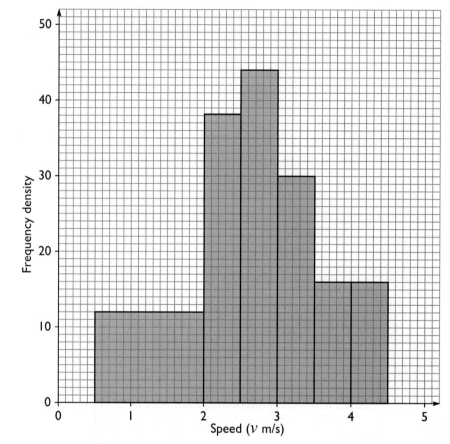

Draw a grouped frequency table for the information in the histogram.

Speed (v m/s)	Frequency density	Class width	Frequency (frequency density × class width)
$0.5 < v \leqslant 2$	12	1.5	18
$2 < v \leqslant 2.5$			
$2.5 < v \leqslant 3$			
$3 < v \leqslant 3.5$			
$3.5 < v \leqslant 4.5$			

DF **5** Fiona recorded the room temperature at 8 a.m. in her office
on each of 90 days. The table gives information about her results.

Room temperature ($x°C$)	Frequency	Class width	Frequency density (frequency ÷ class width)
$10 < x \leqslant 15$	36	5	7.2
$15 < x \leqslant 19$	34	i	ii
$19 < x \leqslant 20$	8	iii	iv
$20 < x \leqslant 22$	12	v	vi

a Find entries for **i**, **ii**, **iii**, **iv**, **v** and **vi** in the table.

b Draw a histogram to represent the data.

DF **6** The cumulative frequency diagram shows information about the magnitudes
of some stars.

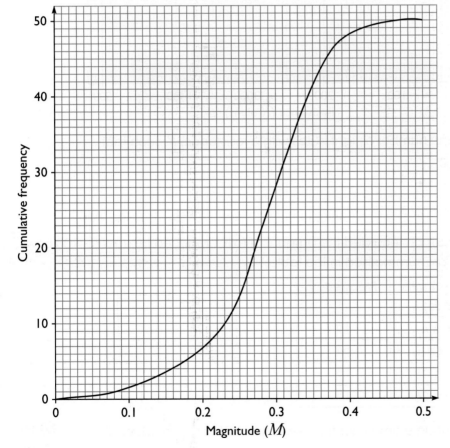

a Find

  i the median magnitude

  ii the interquartile range.

b Draw a histogram for the information in the cumulative frequency
diagram. Use five intervals of equal width.

DF **ES** **7** The histogram gives information about resistances of some light bulbs.

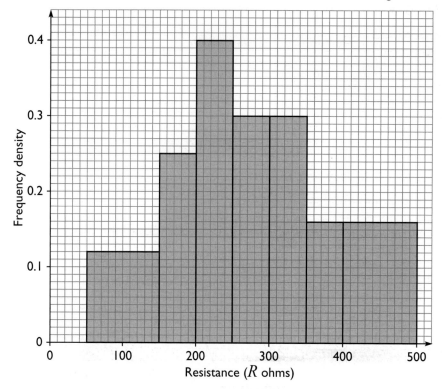

Work out the number of light bulbs with a resistance, R, such that

a $R \leqslant 150$

b $R > 300$

c $160 < R \leqslant 270$

PB **ES** **8** On Friday, Simon recorded the amount of milk produced by each of 100 cows.
His results are summarised in the table.

Amount of milk (a litres)	Frequency
$0 < a \leqslant 4$	15
$4 < a \leqslant 16$	54
$16 < a \leqslant 18$	13
$18 < a \leqslant 26$	18

a Work out an estimate for the mean amount of milk produced.

b Draw a histogram to represent the information in the table.

9 The histogram gives information about the heights, h cm, of a sample of footballers.

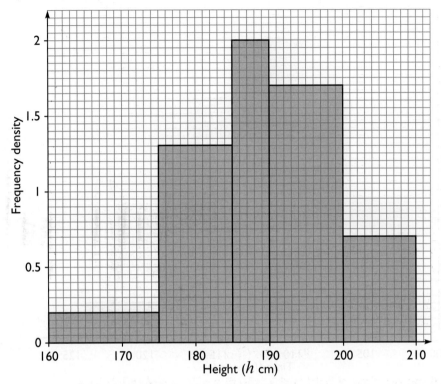

a Work out the total number of footballers in the sample.

b Work out the median height of the footballers.

One of these footballers is selected at random.

c Work out the probability that this footballer has a height greater than 190 cm.

PB **10** Ipeto recorded the times it took some children to run up a hill.
ES The histogram gives some information about these times.

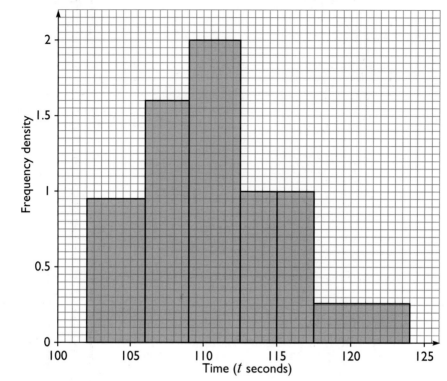

a Work out an estimate for the percentage of these children who took 110 seconds or more to run up the hill.

20% of the children took a time less than T seconds to run up the hill.

b Work out an estimate for T.

Statistics and Probability
Strand 4 Probability Unit 7
Conditional probability

PS PRACTISING SKILLS   **DF** DEVELOPING FLUENCY   **PB** PROBLEM SOLVING   **ES** EXAM-STYLE

PS **1** Tony has

3 red cards numbered 1, 2, 3

4 green cards numbered 1, 2, 3, 4

5 yellow cards numbered 1, 2, 3, 4, 5

Tony takes, at random, a red card, a green card and a yellow card.

How many different possible combinations of cards are there?

PS **2** A bag contains three red beads and five blue beads. Emma is going to take at random two beads from the bag.

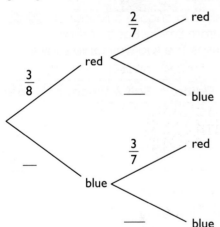

a Copy and complete the probability tree diagram for this information.

b Work out the probability that

  i both beads will be red

  ii both beads will be blue

  iii the first bead will be red and the second bead will be blue.

PS **3** In a survey, 25 students are asked if they are studying Geography and History. The Venn diagram gives information about the results.

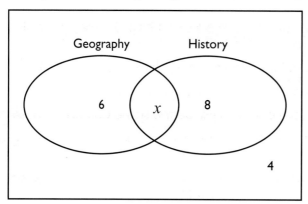

a Work out the value of x.

One of these 25 students is chosen at random.

b Given that this student is studying History, what is the probability that they are also studying Geography?

c Given that this student is studying Geography, what is the probability that they are also studying History?

DF **4** 79 people went on a trip. Each person was asked to choose a flavour of crisps for their lunch box. They could choose from Smoky Bacon crisps, Cheese & Onion crisps and Salt & Vinegar crisps. The two-way table shows information about the choices.

	Smoky Bacon	Cheese & Onion	Salt & Vinegar	Total
Male	15	11	13	39
Female	14	17	9	40
Total	29	28	22	79

Kim selects at random one of these 79 people.

a Given that the person selected is male, what is the probability that he chose Smoky Bacon?

b Given that the person selected chose Salt & Vinegar, what is the probability that they are male?

c Given that the person selected is female, what is the probability that she chose Cheese & Onion or Smoky Bacon?

d Given that the person selected did **not** chose Smoky Bacon, what is the probability that they are female?

DF **5** A box contains only black counters and white counters. A bag contains only black counters and white counters. Jim is going to take at random a counter from the box and a counter from the bag.

The probability that the counter from the box will be white is 0.4. The probability that the counter from the bag will be white is 0.7.

   a Draw a tree diagram to show all the possible outcomes.

   b What is the probability that both counters will be white?

   c What is the probability that both counters will be the same colour?

   d Given that both counters are the same colour, what is the probability that the counter from the box is white?

   e Given that the counters are **not** the same colour, what is the probability that the counter from the bag is black?

DF **6** Danni asked each of 50 people which, if any, of the three qualifying games of a football competition they had watched. Here is some information about her results.

22 had watched Game 1

29 had watched Game 2

14 had watched Game 3

5 had watched Game 1 and Game 3

7 had watched Game 2 and Game 3

12 had watched Game 1 and Game 2

3 had watched all three games

   a Draw a Venn diagram to show this information.

   b Danni is going to pick at random one of these 50 people. What is the probability that this person had watched Game 1 or Game 2?

   c Clive picked at random one of these 50 people. Given that this person had watched Game 3, work out the probability they had also watched Game 1.

   d Billy picked at random one of these 50 people. Given that this person had not watched Game 1, work out the probability they had watched Game 2 and Game 3.

PB
ES **7** A box contains three red pencils, four blue pencils and five green pencils. Terry is going to take at random two pencils from the box.

Work out the probability that both pencils will be the same colour.

PB
ES **8** There are 11 girls and 8 boys in a chess club. Jake is going to pick at random a team from the chess club. The team will have two players.

Work out the probability that Jake will **not** pick two boys for the team.

PB **9**
ES

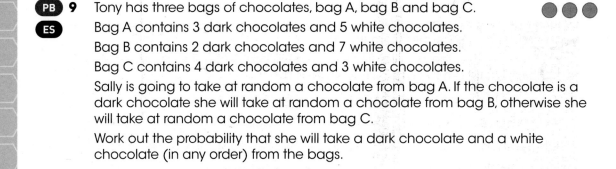

Tony has three bags of chocolates, bag A, bag B and bag C.

Bag A contains 3 dark chocolates and 5 white chocolates.

Bag B contains 2 dark chocolates and 7 white chocolates.

Bag C contains 4 dark chocolates and 3 white chocolates.

Sally is going to take at random a chocolate from bag A. If the chocolate is a dark chocolate she will take at random a chocolate from bag B, otherwise she will take at random a chocolate from bag C.

Work out the probability that she will take a dark chocolate and a white chocolate (in any order) from the bags.

PB **10**
ES

Here are some cards. Each card has a letter on it. Shelly is going to take at random three of these cards.

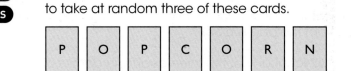

Work out the probability that two of the three cards will have the same letter on them.